FROM SHADOWY TYPES TO TRUTH

FROM SHADOWY TYPES TO TRUTH

Studies in Milton's Symbolism

by William G. Madsen

New Haven and London, Yale University Press, 1968

Copyright © 1968 by Yale University.
Designed by John O. C. McCrillis,
set in Baskerville type,
and printed in the United States of America by
The Carl Purington Rollins Printing-Office of
the Yale University Press, New Haven, Connecticut.
Distributed in Canada by McGill University Press.

Library of Congress catalog card number: 68–13918

FOR RETA

Acknowledgments

Parts of this book were given as papers at meetings of the Modern Language Association and the English Institute and were subsequently published in *PMLA*, *SEL*, and *The Lyric and Dramatic Milton,* ed. Joseph H. Summers (New York and London, Columbia University Press, 1965). I am grateful for permission to reprint.

Most of my research was done while I was the holder of a Morse Fellowship from Yale University, and most of the writing was made possible by summer research grants from Wayne State University and Emory University. I am deeply grateful to the faculty fellowship and research committees of these three universities.

My general indebtedness to Milton scholars and critics will be apparent. More particularly, I have received advice and encouragement from Arthur E. Barker, Douglas Bush, Davis P. Harding, Merritt Y. Hughes, Walter MacKellar, Ralph Nash, Joseph H. Summers, and Kester Svendsen. The names of Louis L. Martz and the late E. E. Stoll are omitted from this list because my debt to them is a more special one. It was to their living voices that I hearkened when I began my study of Milton, and I am content to have no better guides.

WILLIAM G. MADSEN

Atlanta
July 1967

Note on Citations

Citations from Milton's poetry are to *John Milton: Complete Poems and Major Prose,* ed. Merritt Y. Hughes (New York, Odyssey Press, 1957). Citations from Milton's prose, unless otherwise noted, are to *The Student's Milton,* ed. Frank Allen Patterson (rev. ed. New York, F. S. Crofts & Co., 1941), abbreviated *SM* in the notes.

Contents

FROM SHADOWY TYPES TO TRUTH

1

Introduction

The contemporary critical interest in imagery, metaphor, and symbol has greatly improved our understanding of Milton's poetry. We no longer think of his use of classical materials as merely decorative, and we have become accustomed to look for themes that are not explicitly stated but are implicitly contained in large symbolic patterns. In *L'Allegro* and *Il Penseroso,* for example, the imagery of light and sound has been shown to imply a gradual progression from the merely natural activities of the first poem (symbolized by the movement from day to night and by the references to melodic or horizontal music) to the supernatural vision of the second (symbolized by the movement from night to day and by the final reference to harmonic or vertical music).[1] The symbolic structures of the *Nativity Ode, Lycidas, Comus,* and even *Arcades* have been analyzed, and of course *Paradise Lost* has also been examined, though not so exhaustively, from this point of view.[2]

1. Don Cameron Allen, *The Harmonious Vision* (Baltimore, 1954), pp. 3–23.
2. The main directions of recent criticism are well exemplified in two anthologies: Arthur E. Barker, ed., *Milton: Modern Essays in Criticism* (New York, 1965), hereafter cited as Barker; and C. A. Patrides, ed., *Milton's* Lycidas: *The Tradition and the Poem* (New York, 1961), hereafter cited as Patrides.

1

Some critics have addressed themselves to the question of whether Milton's use of symbols implies a particular view of the nature of reality and of the relation of language to that reality. A view that was more common twenty years ago than it is today, though it still appears, is that Milton's philosophical and religious commitment did not permit him to use symbols at all and that Milton the poet is thus at odds with Milton the Puritan. Probably the most prevalent view today is that Milton's use of symbols is a function of his Neoplatonic belief that earth is the "shadow of Heav'n," that physical realities, because of the nature of the universe, are images of a higher reality which the poet seeks to embody in his poem. The thesis of this book is that Milton's symbolic theory and practice can best be understood in the context of theories of biblical interpretation that were current in his day, and, in particular, that the doctrine of typology throws more light on the symbolic structure of the major poems as well as on Milton's philosophical and religious presuppositions than do the currently fashionable theories about metaphoric or mythic structure and Neoplatonic *allegoria*. The chapters that follow will discuss various aspects of the theory of typology.[3] Here I want merely to define it briefly and explore its relevance to *Lycidas*.

In its narrowest sense the theory of typology states that

3. Two recent theological studies are G. W. H. Lampe and K. J. Woollcombe, *Essays on Typology* (London, 1957), and Jean Daniélou, *From Shadows to Reality*, trans. Wulstan Hibberd (Westminster, Md., 1960).

certain persons, things, and events of the Old Testament are symbolic prefigurations, "shadows," or types of certain persons, things, and events of the New Testament. Thus Joshua is a type of Christ, who is the antitype; the synagogue a type of the Christian Church; the sacrifice of Isaac a type of the Crucifixion. Sometimes the antitypes are not limited to the New Testament but extended to the whole Christian Church and its members. The exodus of the Jews from Egypt to the Promised Land was commonly regarded as a type of the journey of every Christian soul from the fleshpots of this world through the wilderness of self-denial and suffering to the Promised Land of Heaven. Some theologians have regarded certain persons and events of the New Testament as types whose antitypes are to be found in the future history of the Church. The method can even be extended beyond the confines of the Bible to encompass pagan history and literature. Dante regarded the Roman Empire as a foreshadowing of the Christian Church and Empire, and Renaissance Neoplatonists were fond of seeing in Hercules a type of Christ and in pagan sacrifices a foreshadowing of the Mass.[4]

Typological interpretation of the Old Testament was universally practiced by both Protestants and Catholics in Milton's day, but it gradually fell into abeyance in the eighteenth and nineteenth centuries. It has recently en-

---

4. Charles Till Davis, *Dante and the Idea of Rome* (Oxford, Clarendon Press, 1957), pp. 233–35; Frances Yates, *The French Academies of the Sixteenth Century* (London, Warburg Institute, 1947), pp. 191–92, 172–73.

joyed a revival among theologians, although there is no general agreement about how it is to be applied or even about its validity as a mode of interpretation. Some modern theologians reject it altogether; others would limit the Old Testament types to those explicitly mentioned in the New Testament; a minority feel free to exercise their own critical judgment or ingenuity. We need not concern ourselves here with the technical rules for discovering types laid down by theologians. The following observations, derived from a study of the types commonly accepted by Milton's contemporaries, will be sufficient for our literary purpose:

A type is a historical person or event, not a mythical person or a recurrent event, such as the rising and setting of the sun.[5]

A type looks forward in time, not upward through the scale of being. The theory of typology is thus firmly grounded in the Judaeo-Christian philosophy of existence and is fundamentally alien to the Greek philosophy of essences.

Natural objects may be types but usually only in special historical circumstances. St. Paul says that the rock that Moses struck was Christ (the water that issued forth was regarded as a type of the blood and

5. See Jean Daniélou, "The Problem of Symbolism," *Thought,* 25 (1950), 423–40, for an illuminating discussion of the relation between cosmic symbolism and typological symbolism in Christian thought and expression.

4

water that flowed from Christ's side when it was pierced by the spear); this does not mean that every rock is a type of Christ.

There must be both similarities and differences between a type and its antitype.

Neither the actors of a typical event nor the authors of their history understand the typological significance of what they are doing or writing. The Jews wandering in the wilderness did not know that manna prefigured the Eucharist, nor did Joshua know that in leading his people into the Promised Land he was a type of Jesus leading His people into Heaven.

Hence, the meaning of a type cannot be known until it has been fulfilled in its antitype.

If these rules are kept in mind, it will be easy enough to distinguish between type or "shadow," on the one side, and allegory, metaphor, image, and literary symbol, on the other, however difficult it may be to distinguish among the latter. In the next chapter I shall discuss in some detail the distinctions that were made by Scholastic and Reformation theologians; before examining the typological symbolism in *Lycidas,* however, it is necessary to insist on the difference between type and metaphor.

A metaphor is a *word* used in other than its literal sense; a type is a *person, thing,* or *event* that prefigures a future person, thing, or event. The speaker of a metaphor is aware of the metaphorical intention of what he says; in Old Testament typology, only the Divine Author of the sacred history (both acted and written) is aware at the time of a symbolic or typological intention.

Literary scholars who are familiar with the theory of typology have largely contented themselves with explaining to twentieth-century readers ignorant of the tradition what some of the standard Old Testament types are and explicating poems in which references to these types appear. The reader of Rosemond Tuve's *A Reading of George Herbert*,[6] to take the outstanding example of this kind of scholarship in English literature, will find that his understanding of Herbert's poetry has been enriched by the wealth of illustrative material that Miss Tuve provides. Compared to Herbert, however, Milton makes but sparing use of the standard types, and it hardly seems necessary to erect an elaborate typological scaffolding simply to explain the references to Pan and Hercules in the *Nativity Ode*. The relevance of the theory of typology to Milton's poetry lies in the fact that Milton employed typology not as a dictionary of ready-made symbols but as a mode of discourse. Let us look at *Lycidas* from this perspective.

The central problem in *Lycidas* is the question of mode of discourse (and the related question of unity of tone) raised by Dr. Johnson.

> We know that they never drove a field, and that they had no flocks to batten; and though it be allowed that

6. Chicago, 1952. The classic studies are of course those of Erich Auerbach, esp. *Mimesis* (Princeton, 1953), passim, and "Figura," in *Scenes from the Drama of European Literature* (New York, 1959), pp. 11–76.

6

the representation may be allegorical, the true meaning is so uncertain and remote that it is never sought because it cannot be known when it is found. . . .

This poem has yet a grosser fault. With these trifling fictions ["a long train of mythological imagery, such as a college easily supplies"] are mingled the most awful and sacred truths, such as ought never to be polluted with such irreverend combinations. The shepherd likewise is now a feeder of sheep, and afterwards an ecclesiastical pastor, a superintendent of a Christian flock. Such equivocations are always unskilful; but here they are indecent, and at least approach to impiety, of which, however, I believe the writer not to have been conscious.[7]

The prevailing critical view of the "irreverend combinations" that Johnson complained of is that, far from being "trifling fictions," the pagan deities and mythological images are transparent symbols of Christian truths. Thus we have been taught to regard Orpheus as a foreshadowing of Christ as well as an example of the poet-priest, and in various aspects of the landscape (the evergreens, the waters that sink beneath the earth only to rise again) we may see symbols of immortality or of death and rebirth. The logic of this position requires, however, that one find a Christian meaning for every classical reference or else admit quite frankly that the poem lacks organic unity because it con-

7. Dr. Johnson's discussion of *Lycidas* (from *Lives of the Poets*) is reprinted in Patrides, pp. 56–57.

tains merely decorative elements. Some of the efforts to save the poem's unity are desperate: the lines about the "fatal and perfidious Bark," which strike the uninstructed reader as the purest paganism, turn out to be a reference to original sin, and the plaintive appeal to pagan mythology in "O ye dolphins, waft the hapless youth" is an appeal to Christ (of whom the dolphin is a type) to convey Lycidas' body safely to Heaven.[8] The nymphs are harder to deal with, since no one apparently has ever suggested that they foreshadow Christ, but the critics are not without their resources. It appears that Milton put the nymphs in the poem simply to deny their existence. The speaker asks them where they were but does not stay for an answer; instead he says they could not have done any good anyway. If they were not there, and if they could not have helped even if they had been, they must not exist.[9] By this device, it would seem, Milton not only has his cake and eats it, but manages to get some pretty decorative frosting on it as well.

A fatal drawback in almost all these symbolic studies of *Lycidas* is that they treat the poem as if it were a painting or a musical composition. Those who seem to regard it as a painting speak of patterns of imagery and of symbolic structure, and in its beginning they see its end. The way to experience the poem, apparently, is to see it all at once, as Mozart is said to have heard the Hafner symphony. In

8. Michael Lloyd, "The Fatal Bark," *MLN*, 75 (1960), 103–09; Northrop Frye, "Literature as Context: Milton's *Lycidas*," in Patrides, p. 202.

9. *Poems of Mr. John Milton,* ed. Cleanth Brooks and John Edward Hardy (New York, 1951), p. 174.

this view the dimension of time in which the poem moves is quite illusory: there is no reason for us to be surprised when we reach the consolation because we knew from the very first mention of laurels and ivy that Lycidas was not dead. If we happen not to notice the laurels and the ivy, we certainly cannot miss, right in the center of the picture, the gory visage of Orpheus sent down the swift Hebrus to the Lesbian shore. Other critics, less capable perhaps of angelic modes of apprehension, prefer musical analogies. They speak of emotional rhythm, of harmony and discord, of modulations of tone and resolutions of despair. Notes of grief alternate with notes of affirmation, and the flower passage, for example, modulates between the strident dissonance of St. Peter's denunciation and the exultant diapason of the consolation. This kind of interpretation has the advantage of regarding the poem as dynamic, as moving in time, but it ignores the fact that it is made up of words spoken by persons, not of disembodied sounds played on an instrument.

To my knowledge the only recent critic who has consistently regarded *Lycidas* as speech is Meyer Abrams. Without rejecting the valuable insights of earlier critics, Abrams insists that up to the last eight lines, which are spoken by Milton as omniscient narrator, the poem is spoken by an uncouth swain who not only speaks in his own person but also reports the speeches of others. Abrams then attempts to relate some of the patterns of imagery and symbol seen by earlier critics to the psychology of the uncouth swain, but instead of speaking of emotional ebb and flow,

9

of modulation of tone and resolution of discord, he speaks of "a gradual shift from the natural, pastoral, and pagan viewpoint to the viewpoint of Christian revelation"; the movement of *Lycidas,* he says, is "patently from despair through a series of insights to triumphant joy."[10] Abrams is certainly right in regarding the uncouth swain as a persona distinct from Milton, but his view that the swain ascends gradually from the grief-stricken pagan pastoralism of the opening to the exultant Christian pastoralism of the consolation is, I think, psychologically unconvincing, for it fails to offer a satisfactory explanation of the flower passage.

The flower passage has ensnared most of the critics, and there is little agreement about its function or emotional tone. For David Daiches it is an attempt to "transmute the dead Lycidas into something beautiful and fragrant." For J. E. Hardy its function is ironic. It is "false surmise" to suppose that nature can offer any comfort, for "nature is neutral: it does not participate in grief for the dead man." Similarly Wayne Shumaker speaks of the passage as "too pretty-pretty, too conventionally poetic to carry a heavy emotional weight." In this context, he says, it is "consciously and deliberately delusive." The words "consciously" and "deliberately" imply some kind of rational control, but apparently Shumaker does not really mean this, for he goes on to say that because the flower passage is delusive it is followed by a mood of "profound spiritual depression; and this, by a natural emotional rhythm, illustrated on the abnormal level by the familiar manic-depressive pattern,

10. "Five Types of *Lycidas,*" in Patrides, p. 226.

passes into the final rapture." Rosemond Tuve and Don Cameron Allen, on the other hand, regard the flower passage as affirmative and even exultant in tone. There is in this passage, says Miss Tuve, a "sense that there is such a thing as loving pity in the natural universe," which, "seeping in after the inimical violence which preceded, becomes a calm strong tide carried by the generous abandon of these lines."[11] For Allen the tide is strong but not calm. The flower passage marks the point where philosophy bows to theology. "The fact of death becomes truly unimportant and the world which had been dead, dry, colorless, and stagnant comes bursting into life. In similar wise, the waters of life, which had rotted or lain almost without motion, race in their currents and thunder in their roaring. . . . The poem now swirls towards a mystical conclusion."[12]

Abrams rejects these analogies to painting, music, abnormal psychology, and hydrodynamics. Instead, he tries to relate the flower passage to the "evolving thought" of the uncouth swain. The resolution of the elegy is assured in St. Peter's speech, he says, because in it "Christ, the shepherd who dies to be born again, is paralleled to the dead shepherd Lycidas, though by allusion only." But "the elegiac singer," he continues,

> is momentarily occupied with the specific references rather than the Scriptural overtones of Peter's com-

11. The quotations from Daiches, Hardy, Shumaker, and Tuve will be found in Patrides, pp. 115, 148, 127, and 193.
12. *The Harmonious Vision*, pp. 68–69.

11

ment, with the result that the resolution, so skill-
fully planted in his evolving thought, is delayed until
he has tried to interpose a little ease by strewing imaginary flowers on Lycidas' imagined hearse. But this
evasion only brings home the horror of the actual
condition of the lost and weltering corpse. By extraordinary dramatic management, it is at this point of
profoundest depression that the thought of Lycidas'
body sinking to "the bottom of the monstrous world"
releases the full implication of St. Peter's speech, and
we make the leap from nature to revelation, in the
great lyric peripety: "Weep no more woful Shepherds
weep no more."[13]

This interpretation is not convincing. If we are to suppose
that the speaker suddenly realizes the scriptural overtones
of St. Peter's speech, then we must assume that he is a
Christian well versed in the New Testament. But if he is a
Christian, why does he sound so much like a pagan? Why
does he turn to nature for consolation? Why does he question the nymphs? Why is he satisfied with the pagan super-
stition that

> It was that fatal and perfidious Bark
> Built in th'eclipse, and rigg'd with curses dark,
> That sunk so low that sacred head of thine[?]

How can the person who plaintively and ineffectually calls
on the dolphins to waft the hapless youth suddenly speak

13. Patrides, pp. 228–29.

with the unambiguous accent of authority? The answer, I suggest, is that he cannot. The current confusion about *Lycidas* has resulted from assuming that the consolation is spoken by the uncouth swain. We have failed to hear the voice of Michael.

If we disregard the speeches of Phoebus and the pilot of the Galilean lake and read only those passages in which the uncouth swain speaks in his own person, we will see that up to the consolation he does not progress one iota from the "natural, pastoral, and pagan viewpoint" of the opening. Besides that, there is a kind of dogged insistence in his devotion to pastoralism. After hearing the higher strain of Phoebus he turns to Greek and Latin pastoral poetry— Arethuse and Mincius—and listens to the herald of the Sea and sage Hippotades, who can explain the inexplicable only by referring to "curses dark." After the "dread voice" of the pilot of the Galilean lake (whose identity there is no need to suppose the uncouth swain aware of), he bids Alpheus return and asks the Sicilian muse to "call the Vales, and bid them hither cast / Their Bells and Flowrets of a thousand hues." But the waters that return are not the waters of Alpheus; they are the "sounding Seas" and the "whelming tide" that have hurled the bones of Lycidas we know not where. Little wonder that the speaker in his despair cries for pity; little wonder that he hopes for a kind of pagan miracle, imploring the dolphins to waft the hapless youth. This is indeed a point of profound spiritual depression. It is where philosophy bows to theology, where grace takes over from nature, where the lyric peripety occurs.

But it does not occur in the void or in the mind of the uncouth swain because he suddenly realizes the implications of the Galilean pilot's speech. It occurs because the angel does indeed melt with ruth and reveal to the uncouth swain that there are "other groves, and other streams" than those of the pastoral tradition.

Assigning the Christian consolation to Michael preserves the formal symmetry of the poem, since each of the three major sections now ends with a speaker other than the uncouth swain. It also makes unnecessary the desperate attempts to find a Christian significance for every pagan image. We are free to assign to the deities and nymphs whatever literal or metaphoric meaning we suppose the uncouth swain to have intended. Having thus established a literal level of meaning (in biblical interpretation, as we shall see, the literal level includes metaphors and allegories intended by the human author), we can superimpose upon it our fuller Christian understanding, as Milton himself did when he read the Old Testament, and we can see what the uncouth swain could not see—that the fragmentary symbols of rebirth and immortality scattered throughout the pastoral landscape are gathered up into the perfect image of Christ and given significance only because He really did rise from the dead. In other words, when we speak of Christian significance in *Lycidas* we are dealing with typological symbolism, not metaphor.

In applying the theory of typology to a reading of *Lycidas*, I am of course using the word "typological" analogously, in a way that Milton and his contemporaries probably would not have used it. The historical reality of the types in the Bible was taken for granted by them; *Lycidas* is only a fiction. When we read the poem typologically we assume that Milton is treating the fiction of a pagan shepherd turning to his sources of consolation as if that fiction were historically true. By so doing, he converts the pastoral tradition to Christian use, as the Old Testament was converted to Christian use. When Milton read the Old Testament, he did not regard everything in it as typological; at the same time, he regarded it as the record of God's preparation for the coming of Christ by raising His Chosen People "From shadowy Types to Truth." Thus when reading *Lycidas,* we need not regard every pagan allusion as a symbol or foreshadowing of Christ; on the other hand, we need not regard them as merely ornamental. By not committing himself to using only those pastoral images that can be given an immediate Christian reference, Milton maintains both the rich particularity of the pastoral tradition and the organic unity of his Christian poem and provides the tension necessary to keep the pagan and Christian symbols apart. To adapt W. K. Wimsatt's description of a poem as the context "which keeps a metaphor alive, that is, which holds the focal terms A and B in such a way that they remain distinct and illuminate each other, instead of collapsing into literalness,"[14] we may say that in *Lycidas* Milton creates a context which keeps pagan types and Christian antitypes from collapsing. The poem is both dynamic and static, analogous both to drama and to painting. On the literal level it is a dramatic structure moving

14. *The Verbal Icon* (New York, 1958), p. 128.

from grief to joy and containing a kind of lyric peripety, as Abrams suggests, and on the typological level it is a pattern of images in which the end is implicit in the beginning.

The voice of the swain perhaps returns with the lines

> Now *Lycidas,* the Shepherds weep no more;
> Henceforth thou art the Genius of the shore,
> In thy large recompense, and shalt be good
> To all that wander in that perilous flood.

The regularity of the couplets, after the metrical variations of the swain's earlier lines, mirrors his calmness of mind after Michael's revelation that Lycidas is not dead, while the classical terminology betrays his as yet imperfect comprehension of what he has heard. Be that as it may, the last eight lines are spoken by Milton in his own person, as Abrams suggests, but on the literal level they have nothing to do with Milton's rededication of himself after having been purged of doubt and despair. They tell instead of the full effect of Michael's speech on the uncouth swain, who now sings with a new voice and sees with new eyes. Pastoral song and pastoral landscape have been transfigured for him. With the voice of Michael telling of other groves and other streams still ringing in his ears, he will turn tomorrow to fresh woods and pastures new.

Lycidas is a pivotal work in Milton's poetic and intellectual development. The mind of the youthful Milton strikes one as that of an extremely gifted but still typical Renaissance Christian humanist with a decided Platonic or Neoplatonic bent. Although it seems a disservice to *Comus* to read it as a full-fledged allegory of the Plotinian descent and ascent of the soul,[15] the mask is certainly strongly tinged with Neoplatonism, and the same may be said of some of the *Prolusions* and *Il Penseroso*. In the earlier elegies there is a collapsing of the pagan and the Christian that suggests at least a partial acceptance of the syncretizing tendencies of the Florentine school of Neoplatonism. In *Lycidas* the pagan myths are still there, functioning in a way that will be impossible for Milton in *Paradise Lost* and *Paradise Regained,* but at the same time the method of *Lycidas,* if I have read the poem correctly, looks ahead to the later poems. A *Lycidas* written at an earlier age, I suggest, would have employed the same kind of transparent symbolism that Spenser employed in the May Eclogue and that enabled E. K. to say, *"Great Pan* is Christ, the very God of all shepheards." In *Lycidas* Orpheus is not Christ. By creating what may be called a typological context—that is, a context in which literal statements *acquire* a metaphoric or symbolic dimension because of a revelatory development in the narrative—Milton is able to forgo the allegorical "veils" and literal "shells" that enclose spiritual "nutmeats" of Renaissance theory[16] without losing any of the deeper and higher resonances he desired.

15. Sears Jayne, "The Subject of Milton's Ludlow *Mask," PMLA, 74* (1959), 533–43. Reprinted in Barker.

16. For an elaborate statement of the poetry as veil doctrine see Leone Ebreo, *The Philosophy of Love (Dialoghi d'Amore),* trans. F. Friedeberg-Seeley and Jean H. Barnes, with an intro. by Cecil Roth (London, 1937), pp. 110–14. Other references will be found in Charles G. Osgood, *Boccaccio on Poetry* (New York, 1956 [Princeton, 1930]), p. 157, n.8, and Index, s.v. Poetry, a veil.

2

Theories of Biblical Interpretation

In assuming the role of inspired narrator in *Paradise Lost*
Milton makes a bold claim to "see and tell / Of things invisible to mortal sight" (III.54–55). I am not presently
concerned with the question "What did the poet see?";
partial answers to it may be found in almost anything that
has been written about *Paradise Lost,* and the total answer
is the poem itself in all its possible complexity of meaning.
Part of the answer, of course, is bound up with the other
question that Milton's simple formula demands of us:
"How did the poet choose to tell what he saw?" Or, from
the point of view of the reader, "How are we to interpret
the language with which the poet communicates his
vision?"

Twentieth-century critics have addressed themselves to
this question with increasing frequency and subtlety. W. J.
Grace's bald statement that Milton believed he was "add-
ing historic details to the Scriptures" has found little
acceptance; Isabel MacCaffrey's formula is more cautious:
"The claim for the truth of events is absolute: these things
happened; for the truth of images—the poem's places and
personages—less absolute, but still insistent that the qualities and potencies bodied forth in them are real." A more

popular view is that Milton adopted the method of "accommodation."[1] Just as the Holy Spirit accommodated His language to the rude understandings of the Old Testament Jews, and Raphael his description of the War in Heaven to Adam's understanding, so Milton has accommodated his extraordinary vision to the understanding of ordinary mortals. Hanford, in a classic article that is still widely quoted, combined the theory of accommodation with the Neoplatonic doctrine that truth must be veiled in myth and allegory when he suggested that Milton thought of himself as a kind of Moses Anglicus, "a revealer of truth in the Platonic sense" "representing the 'ideas' to human apprehension [as] only the poet-seer who had looked on the face of truth unveiled could . . . represent them," that is to say, by "poetic myth" and "symbolic images."[2] Recently a more subtle version of the theory of accommodation has appeared, in which it is suggested that "the rhetorical magnificence of *Paradise Lost* depends upon a belief that sense images can convey divine truth only in a world where the

1. W. J. Grace, "Orthodoxy and Aesthetic Method in *Paradise Lost* and the *Divine Comedy*," *CL, 1* (1949), 174; Isabel Gamble MacCaffrey, Paradise Lost *as "Myth"* (Cambridge, Mass., 1959), p. 21. (It is hard to believe that Milton would have made an absolute claim that all the events in *Paradise Lost* really happened.) For the theory of accommodation see Roland M. Frye, *God, Man, and Satan* (Princeton, 1960), pp. 7–13, and C. A. Patrides, *"Paradise Lost* and the Theory of Accommodation," *TSLL, 5* (1963), 58–63.

2. James Holly Hanford, " 'That Shepherd Who First Taught the Chosen Seed': A Note on Milton's Mosaic Inspiration," *UTQ, 8* (1939), 403–19. The quotation in the text is from Hanford's *A Milton Handbook* (4th ed. New York, 1946), p. 227.

natural and supernatural have not fallen apart; only in a world that is not fallen."[3] This latter view implies the conviction, openly stated by a whole school of critics, that as a Puritan Milton had no business using images at all and that the "bare, abstract" style of the last books of *Paradise Lost* and of *Paradise Regained* and *Samson Agonistes* bears witness to the surrender of his Christian humanism to the antipoetic principles of Puritanism. Here we are at the edge of the lunatic fringe, where it is an article of faith that *Paradise Lost,* in its symbolic dimension, is a lie and a cheat.[4]

My own approach to the problems raised by Milton's modes of discourse in *Paradise Lost,* which will be by way of theories of biblical interpretation, may seem to lie across a vast Serbonian bog, but I am emboldened to present the material in this chapter by the contemporary interest in the relation of biblical interpretation to medieval and Renaissance literature and by my conviction that it is better for literary scholars to know too much about theories of biblical interpretation than too little.

The Egypt of Allegory

Typological interpretation of the Old Testament forms a part of the medieval theory of hermeneutics called the fourfold method. It does not necessarily imply this theory, however, and Protestant theologians devoted a good deal

3. R. L. Brett, *Reason and Imagination* (London, 1960), p. 36.
4. See below, pp. 105–06, 166–67.

of energy to disengaging the theory of typology from the Catholic doctrine of the "mystical sense" of Scripture. Before setting out to explore the semantic jungle of sixteenth- and seventeenth-century hermeneutics, it will be well to look at the landmarks provided by Aquinas, whose system may be conveniently summarized in outline form.[5]

Literal sense
  A. Proper
  B. Improper or figurative
    1. Typical (the individual represents the universal)
    2. Parabolic or allegorical (in the grammatical sense)
    3. Moral (as in animal fables)
Spiritual or allegorical sense
  A. Allegorical or typical (to be distinguished from B-1 above), where the Old Testament prefigures the New
  B. Tropological or moral
  C. Anagogical (relating to "eternal glory")

According to Aquinas, the literal meaning resides in the signification of the words used by the human author and thus includes such devices as metaphor, parable, and allegory, while the spiritual meaning resides in the things or events which are signified by the words. The spiritual

5. Adapted from Edgar de Bruyne, *Études D'Esthétique Médiévale* (3 vols. Brugge, Belgium, 1946), 2, 312–13.

sense is based on the literal and presupposes it.[6] A corollary of this definition is that, since only God in His Providence can order events in the historical order in such a way that they will have prophetic significance, it is impossible for literary works other than the Bible to have many meanings.[7]

The sharp precision of Aquinas' thought is somewhat blurred by the inadequacy of his vocabulary, nowhere more apparent than in the word "allegory," which has here three applications. It can mean what Dante called "allegory of the poets," e.g. the *Psychomachia*, the *Roman de la Rose*, or *Pilgrim's Progress*. It can refer generically to the spiritual or mystic sense of Scripture, and it can refer specifically to one kind of spiritual sense, the typological. Sixteenth- and seventeenth-century theorists made a heroic effort to delimit the meaning of "allegory" and with some degree of success, but their semantic distinctions, together with Aquinas' distinction in thought, were lost sight of in the general decay of biblical hermeneutics in the eighteenth and nineteenth centuries, as the confusion in modern terminology attests.

Catholic theologians in the sixteenth and seventeenth centuries refined, extended, and sometimes modified Aquinas' formulations. Whether a reaction against the excesses of late medieval exegetical practice or because of

---

6. *Summa Theologica*, I, Q. 1, Art. 10.

7. *Quaestiones Quodlibetales*, ed. R. P. Mandonnet (Paris, 1926), Quodlibetum 7, Q. VI, Art. 16.

the attacks by the Reformers, their treatises recommend the utmost caution in interpreting the Bible in a mystical sense, and they insist (along with Jerome, Augustine, and Aquinas) on the absolute primacy of the literal meaning. They were at one with the Protestants in this, as Bellarmine pointed out, as well as in their insistence that Christian doctrine could not be proved by mystical interpretations. At the same time, however, they insisted on the principle of multiple meanings.

One of the fullest expositions of Catholic principles of interpretation is to be found in Ferdinand de Escalante's *Clypeus Concionatorum Verbi Dei,* published in 1611 and recommended in Wilkins' *Ecclesiastes.* After stating the familiar position that the literal sense is what the words signify, the spiritual sense what is signified by the things, Escalante says that although every passage in Scripture has a literal sense, not every passage has a spiritual sense. For example, when Scripture warns us against vices, the literal meaning is a moral one and there is no tropological sense. In metaphorical passages the literal sense is what the words signify figuratively. The literal sense has two principal uses: to explain divine doctrines and combat heretics (Escalante quotes the pseudo-Dionysius to the effect that "Symbolica seu mystica theologia non est argumentativa") and to provide the basis for the other senses. If the literal sense is not discovered and firmly established, the spiritual senses will be empty, futile, imaginary, and often false, as in the interpretations of Origen and other heretics, for example. Anyone with a quick wit can fashion spiritual senses, but only learned men thoroughly versed in Scripture can discover the literal sense.[8]

The spiritual sense has four uses. First, all the mysteries of Christ and of the Gospel prefigured in the Old Testament are revealed by means of it; second, it places a veil over the mysteries of the faith lest they be exposed to the unfaithful and scorned; third, without it many of the Mosaic laws would seem puerile, especially in comparison with the praiseworthy laws of Solon or Lycurgus; and fourth, many of the Old Testament stories of incest, sacrilege, and adultery are unedifying unless interpreted spiritually. There are two kinds of spiritual sense, those devised by man's own wit and those intended by God. The first kind are often vague and uncertain, but they are not to be despised if they do not contradict divine or human truth, if they are conducive to piety, if sacred things are not used to adorn profane (as in the interpretations of Pico), and if they are not taken from the bare words but from the things signified by the words, insofar as these things bear a similitude to something else. The spiritual senses intended by God are of course certain and may be used probatively, but it is very difficult to tell what spiritual senses actually were intended by God. Escalante offers five rules for identifying them, among which are the testimony of the New Testament (the most valid for proof, of course) and the testimony of the Fathers.[9]

One of the Protestant objections to the Catholic theory

8. Escalante, col. 78–93.
9. Ibid., col. 100–05.

that there is a mystic or spiritual sense based on the things signified by the words of Scripture is that in metaphor, which Catholics regard as part of the literal sense, it is not the words but the things referred to that carry the significance of the metaphor. In trying to meet this objection Escalante is forced into a position that would not recommend itself to most modern critics. He denies that a metaphor denotes those things which it properly signifies; rather it is transferred to some other thing in such a way that it expresses that thing alone. Thus when we call Christ a lion, the word "lion" does not signify the animal, and the animal Christ; rather the word "lion" refers immediately to Christ.[10] The formulation of Nicolai Serarius, a Jesuit who published a *Prolegomena Bibliaca* in 1612, seems more in keeping with modern ideas of the "transaction" between tenor and vehicle than either Escalante's theory or those of most of his Protestant adversaries. Serarius points out that in a metaphor there is always a similitude and consequently two terms. But it is not necessary, he says, that we understand one term first and then the other. Rather we understand them simultaneously, as related. The metaphorical word signifies primarily and proximately the transferred meaning, but with respect to the thing from which it is transferred and from which the similitude is drawn. Serarius is thus faithful to the nature of metaphor without having to abandon the Catholic position that the spiritual sense of Scripture is based on the

10. Ibid., col. 114–15.

things signified by the words and that metaphor is an example of the improper literal meaning.[11]

Wandering in the Wilderness

The early Reformers made a frontal attack on the medieval theory of the fourfold sense. Although Luther in his own exegesis leaned toward allegorical interpretations, in principle he thought that "The Holy Spirit is the very simplest writer and speaker there is in heaven and earth; therefore His words, too, cannot have more than one most simple sense, which we call the Scriptural or literal or tongue-sense."[12] Tyndale is equally blunt: "Thou shalt understand, therefore, that the Scripture hath but one sense, which is the literal sense. And that literal sense is the root and ground of all, and the anchor that never faileth, whereunto if thou cleave thou canst never err, or go out of the way." Allegories, he says, are the reason we are now in bondage to Antichrist the Pope. Origen started it all, and "then came our sophisters with their anagogical and chopological sense, and with an antitheme of half an inch, out of which some of them draw a thread of nine days long." Tyndale is objecting to allegorical interpretations superimposed on the literal meaning; like all the Reformers he allowed allegorical interpretations in principle if they

11. Serarius, p. 140.
12. Quoted from Luther's *Reply to Esmer* by F. W. Loetscher, "Luther and the Problem of Authority in Religion," *Princeton Theological Review, 16* (1918), 529.

were regarded as "accommodations" of the text rather
than as meanings intended by the author.

> Beyond all this, when we have found out the literal
> sense of the Scripture, by the process of the text, or by
> a like text of another place, then go we, and as the
> Scripture borroweth similitudes of worldly things,
> even so we again borrow similitudes or allegories of
> the Scripture, and apply them to our purposes; which
> allegories are no sense of the Scripture, but free things
> besides the Scripture, and altogether in the liberty of
> the Spirit.[13]

The principle of one literal meaning proved difficult to
apply in all its rigor; indeed, if it had been rigorously applied, the Old Testament would soon have become a
closed book, since (as the Church Fathers had recognized)
the only way to preserve its character as the inspired word
of God and at the same time make it available to Christianity was to interpret it allegorically or spiritually, as the
Stoics had interpreted Homer in order to make him available to a more sophisticated audience. As a matter of fact,
allegorical and typological interpretation of the Old Testament began not with the Fathers but with the authors of
the New Testament, and the early Reformers were hard
put to explain passages such as the following:

---

13. William Tyndale, *The Obedience of a Christian Man,* in *The Works
of the English Reformers: William Tyndale and John Frith,* ed. T.
Russell (3 vols. London, 1831), *1,* 339, 343, 341.

Moreover, brethren, I would not that ye should be ignorant, how that all our fathers were under the cloud, and all passed through the sea;

And were all baptized unto Moses in the cloud and in the sea;

And did all eat the same spiritual meat;

And did all drink the same spiritual drink: for they drank of that spiritual Rock that followed them: and that Rock was Christ. (I Cor. 10:1–4)

For it is written, that Abraham had two sons, the one by a bondmaid, the other by a freewoman.

But he who was of the bondwoman was born after the flesh; but he of the freewoman was by promise.

Which things are an allegory. (Gal. 4:24)

And as Moses lifted up the serpent in the wilderness, even so must the Son of man be lifted up. (John 3:14)

Let no man therefore judge you in meat, or in drink, or in respect of an holyday, or of the new moon, or of the sabbath days:

Which are a shadow of things to come; but the body is of Christ. (Col. 2:17)

There is no problem about the literal meaning of these passages, but what of the Old Testament narrations to which they refer? Having rejected the Catholic position that there is a spiritual meaning in the Old Testament signified by the events themselves, the Protestants had to assert either that St. Paul was merely accommodating the text to his purpose or that the typological meaning was itself the literal meaning. Of the passage in Galatians Calvin said that "Paul certainly does not mean that Moses wrote the history for the purpose of being turned into an allegory, but points out in what way the history may be made to answer the present subject."[14] This is an example of what was commonly called the accommodative meaning. Calvin did not apply the theory of allegorical accommodation to the other examples of typological interpretation in the New Testament, however, and he was driven to the desperate expedient of asserting that the Old Testament types like Jonah, the brazen serpent, and so on referred literally to Christ and were so understod by the Jews.[15]

Melanchthon agrees with Calvin that the typological meaning is the literal meaning, and he says that the verse "Thou art a priest for ever after the order of Melchizedek" refers literally and historically to Christ, not to David at all.[16] Flacius Illyricus quotes Melanchthon with approval in his influential *Clavis Scripturae Sacrae,* published in Basle in 1567, but his own discussion reveals a certain backing away from the logical but untenable position of Calvin and Melanchthon. Flacius distinguishes carefully

14. John Calvin, *Commentaries on The Epistles of Paul to the Galatians and Ephesians,* trans. Rev. William Pringle (Edinburgh, 1841), p. 116.

15. Kemper Fullerton, *Prophecy and Authority* (New York, 1919), pp. 138–39.

16. Melanchthon is quoted to this effect by Flacius Illyricus, *Clavis Scripturae Sacrae* (Jena, 1674 [first pub. 1567]), Altera Pars, col. 67.

between type and allegory. A type consists in a comparison of deeds and is entirely historical; allegory is concerned not so much with deeds as with words. Types speak of Christ and the Church, the Law and the Gospel; they cannot be accommodated to us. Allegory has a broader application and is often applied to our persons either to instruct us or to arouse our sense of piety. A type or figure is something out of the Old Testament that is shown to have prefigured or foreshadowed something in the New. Allegory is the expounding of anything, either from the Old or New Testament, in a new sense. Thus one and the same narration, Flacius says, can be interpreted both typically and allegorically. For example, when David's fight with Goliath is said to foreshadow Christ's conflict with Satan and victory over him, we have a type; when it is said to signify the war between the flesh and the spirit which each one of us experiences in himself, then we have an allegory.[17] The trouble with this is that Flacius is making two distinctions, not one. His first distinction is that types are of deeds, allegories of words. This is essentially Escalante's distinction between allegory of deeds and allegory of words, the first being the spiritual sense, the second a literal-figurative sense. But Flacius cannot accept this implication, and he therefore shifts his ground to say that types refer to Christ and the Church, allegories to men. This distinction is not necessarily incompatible with the first, but Flacius makes it so when he interprets David's battle with Goliath

17. Ibid., col. 76.

allegorically. Since this is presumably not an instance of expounding the words of the narrative in a new sense but of accommodating the actual event to our own spiritual lives, Flacius' first distinction (between deeds and words) breaks down. His whole discussion leaves us in some doubt as to just what he considered the status of types to be. If they are simply an accommodation of the Old Testament and differ only from allegories in being restricted to Christ and the Church, we have a distinction without a difference; if, on the other hand, they are somehow part of the meaning of the Old Testament, then it is hard to see how Flacius can avoid admitting a spiritual sense, since he would certainly not maintain that the literal meaning of David's battle with Goliath was Christ's battle with Satan. As a matter of fact, Flacius is of two minds and never does succeed in resolving the issue. He admits that many happenings and ceremonies in the Old Testament signified something else and that they are therefore allegories. But they are not to be sought out anxiously, and they do not furnish proof in controversial matters; like pictures they make clearer what is proven from more certain texts.[18] What Flacius seems to be saying is that the literal meaning of many Old Testament passages is allegorical, but that we should not try to figure out what that meaning is. We are thus left with two rather paradoxical results of Flacius' attempt to distinguish between type and allegory. First, while the Catholics used the same word to speak of two very different kinds of inter-

18. Ibid., col. 68.

pretation, allegory of things and allegory of words, Flacius carefully distinguishes two words that apply, in the last analysis, to the same kind of interpretation, the accommodative. Second, his insistence that the literal sense is the only sense, coupled with his conviction that the Old Testament speaks throughout of Christ, forces him to assert that in many Old Testament passages the allegorical or typological meaning is the literal meaning and thus to deny after all what most theologians regarded as the literal-historical meaning.

Flacius has been praised by Farrar as giving to the hermeneutic principles of the Reformers "their clearest statement and most systematic development,"[19] but the writings of the great English Protestant controversialist, William Whitaker, exhibit a much more powerful mind at work.[20] Whitaker admits that such things as allegory, anagoge, and tropology are to be found in Scripture, but he denies that they make various senses. "We affirm that there is but one true, proper and genuine sense of scripture, arising from the words rightly understood, which we call the literal: and we contend that allegories, tropologies, and anagoges are not various senses, but various collections from one sense, or various applications and accommoda-

19. F. W. Farrar, *History of Interpretation* (London, 1886), p. 342.

20. William Whitaker, *A Disputation on Holy Scripture,* trans. Rev. William Fitzgerald (Cambridge, Parker Society, 1849). What follows is taken from Q. 5, Chap. 2, pp. 404–07. For a recent discussion of Whitaker see Charles K. Cannon, "William Whitaker's *Disputatio de Sacra Scriptura:* A Sixteenth-Century Theory of Allegory," *HLQ,* 25 (1962), 129–38.

tions of that one meaning." He applies this principle unequivocally to the story of David and Goliath:

> David fought with Goliah. David was a type of Christ, and Goliah of the devil. Therefore, this fight and victory of David may be typically accommodated to denote the combat of Christ with Satan, and his victory. One may also give an allegorical accommodation of the same narrative, thus: David overcame Goliah. So ought we to overcome our passions, which wage a kind of giant war within us against the Spirit of God. I confess that these are true and may be fitly said: but it would be absurd to say that either the one or the other was the sense of this history.

Unlike Flacius, Whitaker leaves no doubt that he regards both these interpretations as accommodations. That does not mean that he regards all types as such, however. He cannot accept either the view that the Old Testament types refer literally to Christ or the view that they are literary allegories, and he is too clear a thinker to rest in obscurity. He therefore tackles the problem head on. Speaking of the passage from Galatians about the two covenants, which Calvin had called an example of allegorical accommodation, Whitaker says that St. Paul is interpreting the narrative typically, not allegorically.

> The sense, therefore, of that scripture is one only, namely, the literal or grammatical. However, the whole entire sense is not in the words taken strictly,

33

but part in the type, part in the transaction itself. In either of these considered separately and by itself part only of the meaning is contained; and by both taken together the full and perfect meaning is completed.

Again, speaking of Canaan as a type of the kingdom of Heaven, he says:

> Yet this is not a twofold sense; but, when the sign is referred to the thing signified, that which was hidden in the sign is more openly expressed. When we proceed from the sign to the thing signified, we bring no new sense, but only bring out into light what was before concealed in the sign. When we speak of the sign by itself, we express only part of the meaning; and so also when we mention only the thing signified: but when the mutual relation between the sign and the thing signified is brought out, then the whole complete sense, which is founded upon this similitude and agreement, is set forth.

By "sign" Whitaker evidently means the thing and not the word, and in this respect his formulation is traditional. Where he differs from the Catholics (as well as from many Protestants) is in regarding the typical significance as residing in the historical event *as narrated in the Bible.* "When we speak of the sign by itself, we express only part of the meaning"; that is to say, when we read the Exodus narrative purely as narrative it obviously has a "meaning." When we read it as a historical narrative written for our instruction, however, we perceive the mutual relation between the event and its typological significance and thus embrace the complete sense. Whitaker's purpose here is not to enunciate a general principle of biblical interpretation, but simply to explain those Old Testament passages that are interpreted typologically in the New. The guarantee that the complete meaning of these passages is the typological one is the statement of the Holy Spirit. But what if this proviso were removed and the principle were applied to other passages, for instance, the account of David's battle with Goliath? Whitaker scoffs at the notion that the literal sense of this history was Christ's victory over Satan, and any other meaning attached to it he regards as simply an accommodation. But what if a pious interpreter were to say that since David is an admitted type of Christ, there is a mutual relation between his battle with Goliath and Christ's with Satan, and that this is the full and complete meaning of this narrative? This is precisely the direction that Protestant hermeneutics took in the *Philologia Sacra* of the Lutheran Solomon Glass.[21]

The Return to Egypt

Like all the Reformers, Glass rejects the Catholic classification of literal, allegorical, tropological, and anagogical, but he is far from rejecting the Catholic principle that Scripture has a spiritual as well as a literal meaning. "The

21. Frankfort and Hamburg, 1653 (first pub. 1623–36). What follows is taken from Bk. I, Pt. I, Tract I, Sec. I, and Bk. II, Pt. I, Tract I, Secs. II–IV.

sense of Holy Scripture is twofold," he says, "literal and spiritual or mystical." The literal sense is that which is proximately and immediately signified by the words, either taken literally or figuratively; the spiritual sense is that which is signified not by the words, but by the things signified by the words. Less than one hundred years after Luther began to lead his people into the desert of the one literal meaning, we are back with the fleshpots of allegory.

Glass even posits a threefold spiritual sense—allegorical, typical, and parabolic, though he says that, strictly speaking, the typical and parabolic should be species under the genus allegory. Allegory in turn is twofold—innate *(innata),* when the allegory is expressly presented in Scripture itself, and inferred *(illata),* when the allegory is inferred by the interpreter. The latter may be either offered *(oblata)* or extorted *(extorta* or *contorta).* Offered allegories are those which have some probable basis in the literal sense and which conform to the analogy of faith. Extorted allegories are those which have no probable basis in the literal sense, or are accommodated to unfitting objects, or do not conform to the analogy of faith, as when Noah's ark and the Song of Songs are absurdly allegorized to apply to the Virgin Mary.

In his discussion of types Glass discards previous classifications as confusing type with either allegory or exemplum, but his own definition is so broad that he lays himself open to the same charge, and he admits that some of his examples, like Paradise and Jerusalem as types of the Church, many would call allegory. He definitely parts company with the early Reformers when he says that types are not limited in their application to the New Testament. He divides types into two main classes, prophetic and historical. Prophetic types can foreshadow any future or present event or moral truth, while historical types are the spiritual sense of Scripture, in which things of the Old Testament, especially the ceremonial precepts and the Jewish priesthood, prefigure and foreshadow things of the New Testament, especially Christ, the antitype of all the legal ceremonies and the kernel of the entire Scripture. As in his classification of allegory, Glass subdivides historical types into innate and inferred. In spite of his elaborate system of classification, however, Glass' principles of typological interpretation, together with his concrete examples, make it very difficult to distinguish between type and allegory. In one of his rules for explicating types he discusses as a type what was universally regarded as a metaphor: a single thing, he says, may be a type and figure of two contrary things; thus the lion is a type of Christ because of its strength and a type of the devil because of its cruelty.

Although Wilkins recommends the *Philologia Sacra* in his *Ecclesiastes,* Glass' work appears not to have been widely influential in seventeenth-century England, whatever may have been its influence in Holland or America.[22] Or-

22. Perry Miller, ed., *Images or Shadows of Divine Things,* by Jonathan Edwards (New Haven, 1948), p. 141, n.30. As Miller points out, Benjamin Keach's *Tropologia: A Key to Open Scripture Metaphors and Types* (London, 1681) is a redaction of Glass. The only other example of Glass'

thodox Protestants, whether Calvinist or Arminian, preferred the simpler formulations of Flacius or the more subtle ones of Whitaker, although most of them abandoned the attempt to establish a verbal distinction between allegory and type. Thus Wilkins says, "There are divers Texts that have a double sense," both "Historicall and Literall" and "Typicall and Allegoricall."[23] Many Protestants rejected the expression "double sense" and spoke instead of the "full sense," as do John Weemse and John White.[24]

By the middle of the seventeenth century the distinction between the Catholic theory of manifold senses and the Protestant theory of the one literal sense had, for all practical purposes, become meaningless. Both sides agreed that only the literal meaning could be used to prove doctrine, that literal-figurative meanings must conform to the analogy of faith, that "typical" passages in the Old Testament had a double meaning, and that various "allegorical accommodations" might be gathered from the text for homiletic purposes even though they were not intended by the author. Protestants' insistence on the one literal meaning, therefore, did not necessarily impoverish their reading

---

influence that has come to my attention is in the discussion of allegory in John Smith's *The Mysterie of Rhetorique Unvail'd* (London, 1657). Miller's discussion of typology in his introduction to *Images or Shadows* is not wholly reliable.

23. *Ecclesiastes* (London, 1646), pp. 9–10.

24. Weemse, *Exercitations Divine* (London, 1632), p. 182; White, *A Way to the Tree of Life* (London, 1647), p. 167.

either of the Bible or of secular literary texts. As a matter of fact, the left-wing Protestants went further than many Catholics were willing to go in reading the Bible allegorically. They justified their practice, as had Origen and many of the early Fathers, by citing St. Paul's statement that "the letter killeth, but the spirit giveth life." Most of the early Reformers, in attacking the doctrine of the fourfold sense, interpreted St. Paul's statement as referring to the opposition between the Law and the Gospel.[25] By 1611 the Catholic Escalante was making exactly the same point in attacking the "spiritual reformer" Sebastian Franck.[26]

Franck illustrates one of the more extreme uses to which the antinomy between the letter and the spirit might be put. For Franck the letter is the written Scripture itself, and the spirit is the divine revelation in the soul of man. The written Scripture is outward and external, transitory and shifting, full of mystery and paradox, and it brings only knowledge, not power. The true Scripture, like the true Church, is within.[27] In a sense, Franck's position was one to which both orthodox Protestants and Catholics could subscribe. The whole of Aquinas' discussion of the figurative (as distinct from the literal) meaning of the ceremonial law of the Old Testament is an exposition of the inward (moral and spiritual) and typological significance of

25. For an excellent discussion of this topic and its relevance to Milton see H. R. MacCallum, "Milton and Figurative Interpretation of the Bible," *UTQ, 31* (1962), 397–99.

26. Escalante, *Clypeus,* p. 86.

27. Rufus Jones, *Spiritual Reformers in the Sixteenth and Seventeenth Centuries* (London, 1914), pp. 60–61.

the precepts.[28] The contrast between the killing letter and the life-giving spirit was a commonplace of orthodox Puritanism. "The Word of God it selfe in the Letter, without the spirituall meaning, and the finger of Gods Spirit to apply it powerfully to our soules and consciences" is not a sufficient rule of life according to Samuel Bolton in *The Saints Sure and Perpetuall Guide*. It is not enough, says John Weemse, to give the grammatical sense of the words in Scripture; you must give "the sense and the spirituall meaning," otherwise Scripture is like a "nut not broken."[29]

Of course Franck and the like-minded spirits who sprang up in England in the 1640s and 1650s, one hundred years after his death, attached a meaning to the opposition between letter and spirit rather different from that of their more orthodox contemporaries. In 1640 Samuel How published *The Sufficiencie of the Spirits Teaching Without Humane-Learning*. How does not go so far as to say that no learned man can understand the spiritual meaning of the word, but he obviously does not think there are many.

> Let men judge what they will though it be the Pope, and all his Councels of Cardinals and Bishops, and the rest of that *learned rabble,* yet they being destitute of the *Spirit,* can give but a *private interpretation* according to the Apostle's mind: whereas if a Man have the *Spirit* of God, though he be a *Pedler, Tinker,*

28. *S.T.*, I–II, Qq. 101–03.

29. Bolton, *A Three-Fold Treatise* (London, 1634), p. 23; Weemse, *Exercitations*, pp. 162–63.

Chimney-sweeper, or COBLER, he may by the helpe of Gods Spirit, give a more *publique interpretation,* then they all.[30]

By "spirit" How means the gift of understanding that God bestows on whom He chooses. Other sectaries meant a good deal more than this, however. They meant that they themselves were already completely spiritual, that they had attained the state of the blessed in Heaven, defined by Aquinas as a state "wherein nothing is believed in as lacking, nothing hoped for as being yet to come" and where nothing in regard to the worship of God will be figurative, that is, mediated by earthly symbols and ceremonies.[31] For John Saltmarsh the New Testament dispensation bears the same relationship to our present state as the Old Testament dispensation did to the New. Baptism, for example, is merely a legal ceremony, like circumcision, and the "word *baptize* is a *figure* Christ uses to express the depth of a spiritual *mystery.*" All such *"ministration[s]* of the creature or of *letter* . . . are but *signs* and *shadows* of *spiritual* things."[32] John Everard, who translated Franck's little treatise on *The Tree of Knowledge of Good and Evil,* says that "Externall Jesus Christ is a *shadow,* a symbole, a figure of the *Internal:* viz. of him *that is to be born within us.* In our souls." Everard's language here is somewhat unguarded, and a little later in this sermon he feels it neces-

---

30. Sig. E1r.

31. *S.T.,* I–II, Q. 103, Art. 3.

32. *Sparkles of Glory, OR, Some Beams of the Morning-Star* (London, 1647), pp. 134, 247.

sary to state unequivocally that he does not deny the literal-historical meaning of the Gospel narrative.

> My beloved, *Herein Lies* The life of the Scriptures;
> Yet do not think that I go about to deny the Letter:
> I hope I shall stand in justification thereof to *the death,* that those things were *Externally* and *Literally acted.* But this I say still, Let us not be content with the Letter *Only;* Friends, Bear me Record, I say, They were All, Actually and Really done in the flesh; but yet I also say, *They were To Teach us,* That the same things are Alwayes In doing: I am so far from having such a thought (as some ignorantly charge me) as if I would make all the Scriptures a Fable, and meerly *Allegorical,* and no such things done: that I wish from my soul, Cursed be those lips, and *for ever* be they *sealed up,* even with the wrath of *Eternal fire,* that shall deny in the least, the truth of the Letter.[33]

The vehemence of Everard's denial is perhaps explained by the fact that in 1647, six years before the first edition of his sermons, Samuel Rutherford had published *"A Survey of the Spirituall Antichrist. Opening* The secrets of *Familisme* and *Antinomianisme* in the Antichristian Doctrine of *John Saltmarsh,* and *Will. Del,* the present Preachers of the Army now in *England,* and of *Robert Town, Tob. Crisp, H. Denne, Eaton,* and others. In which is revealed the rise and spring of *Antinomians, Familists, Libertines,*

33. *The Gospel-Treasury Opened* (London, 1659), The First Part, pp. 55, 89.

Swenck-feldians, Enthysiasts, &c." Rutherford accuses all *"Papists, Antinomians* and *Familists"* of allegorizing Scripture history out of existence. He quotes the following passage from the catechism of one M. Beacon, whom he regards as a Familist:

Q. How long did this suffering last?
A. Till he gave up the Ghost.
Q. Who was crucified hereby?
A. The old man.
Q. What was the old man?
A. The sinfull man.
Q. Is the sinfull man ceased?
A. Yes, in Christ.
Q. How so?
A. He was left nailed on the crosse.

Rutherford admits that Christ's life and death may be expounded spiritually, "but that is no ground for *Papists, Antinomians* and *Familists* to take away all the truth of histories touching Christ."[34] Actually, "the literall and spirituall sense are one and the same and the *Letter* and *Spirit* subordinate, not contrary . . . for *Scripture* hath not two senses, but the grammaticall and native sense that the words offer, without violence or straining of Scripture, is the true meaning of Scripture." This meaning the natural man will understand "with the naturall, literall and star light of meere naturall reason," and the spiritual man

34. Pp. 189–90.

"with the supernaturall, spirituall, and Sunne-light, and spirituall evidence of a Spirit of grace above nature."[35]

Rutherford was not alone in deprecating the new vogue of "monkish allegory." At least five separate attacks were made on the Familists in 1645 and 1646,[36] the most substantial (and most virulent) of which was Thomas Edwards' *Gangraena*. Among the 176 "errors" listed by Edwards in his first edition are the following:

> 1. That the Scriptures cannot be said to be the word of God; there is no Word but Christ, the Scriptures are a dead letter, and no more to be credited then the writings of men, not divine, but humane invention.
>
> . . .
>
> 5. That the holy writings and sayings of *Moses* and the Prophets, of Christ and his Apostles, and the proper Names, Persons and things contained therein are Allegories, and these Allegories are the mystery and spirituall meaning of them.[37]

Although Gerard Winstanley had yet to appear on the scene when Edwards published the first edition of

---

35. P. 312.

36. I have seen [J. Etherington], *A Brief Discovery of the Blasphemous Doctrine of Familisme* (London, 1645); I. G[raunt], *Truths Victory Against Heresie* (London, 1645); Thomas Gataker, *Shadowes Without Substance* (London, 1646); Benjamin Bourne, *The Description and Confutation of Mysticall Antichrist, the Familists* (London, 1646); and Thomas Edwards, *Gangraena* (London, 1646).

37. Pp. 18–19.

44

Gangraena, his pamphlets provide numerous examples of how types can be allegorized out of existence:

> This first man is he, *by whose disobedience many are made sinners,* or by whom the whole Creation is corrupted; Therefore you Preachers, do not you tell the people any more, That a man called *Adam,* that disobeyed about 6000 years ago, was the man that filled every man with sin and filth, by eating an apple. *Rom.* 5.19. For assure yourselves, this *Adam* is within every man and woman; and it is the first power that appears to act and rule in every man.[38]

Winstanley even allegorizes Christ. The account in Scripture of His resurrection, His appearance to the disciples, and His ascension into Heaven "doth point out the mystery of Christs spirituall rising, and the exaltation of his spirituall power over the flesh." The whole Scriptures, in fact, "are but a report of spirituall mysteries, held forth to the eye of flesh in words; but to be seene in the substantiall matter of them by the eye of the Spirit."[39] Unlike Everard, Winstanley explicitly denies the literal-historical reality of the biblical narratives, but there is nothing in his spiritual interpretations that makes it necessary for him to do so. Most Protestant writers found room in their system of hermeneutics for both the literal sense and the spiritual sense, or at least for spiritual "accommodations." But the

38. *The New Law of Righteousnes,* in *The Works of Gerrard Winstanley,* ed. George H. Sabine (Ithaca, N.Y., 1941), p. 176.
39. *Truth Lifting Up Its Head Above Scandals,* in Sabine, p. 116.

45

orthodox insistence that Scripture has only one "litterall, Grammaticall, and genuine sense" sometimes led unsophisticated persons like Winstanley to suppose that the spirit and the letter were incompatible, even though such spiritual interpretations had for centuries been the staple of Christian devotional literature, Catholic and Protestant alike.

Not every allegorical interpretation adheres to the truth of the letter and the analogy of faith, however. Had Edwards and Rutherford read Henry More's *Conjectura Cabbalistica* they would have found a much more insidious attack on the literal sense of Scripture than anything in the Papists and Familists. In the dedicatory epistle to Cudworth, More appeals to the familiar opposition between the letter and the spirit:

> For as many as are born of the *Spirit,* and are not meer sons of the *Letter,* know very well how much the more inward and mysterious meaning of the Text makes for the reverence of the holy Scripture, and advantage of Godlinesse, when as the urging of the bare *literal* sense, has either made or confirmed many an *Atheist.*[40]

It is obvious, however, that More is interested neither in the letter nor in the spirit of the Mosaic narrative, but rather in Neoplatonic fancies about man and the universe. In *The Philosophick Cabbala,* for example, he interprets the story of the Fall in such a way as to rob it of any literal

40. *Conjectura,* sig. A3.

meaning whatsoever. When first created, Adam was "wholly *Ethereal,* and placed in Paradise, that is, in an happy and joyful condition of the Spirit; for he was placed under the invigorating beams of the *divine Intellect,* and the Sun of Righteousnesse then shone fairly upon him."[41] The Tree of Life was the essential will of God; the Tree of Knowledge was Adam's own will. Eve was the feminine faculty of the soul, the affections. The Temptation consisted in Satan persuading Adam to act according to his own will, and his feminine faculty was tickled. Adam's punishment was to descend to earth from the ethereal region:

> At last the *Plastick Power* being fully awakened, *Adams* Soul descended into the prepared matter of the Earth, and in due processe of time *Adam* appear'd cloth'd in the skin of beasts; that is, he became a downright *terrestrial Animal,* and a mortal creature upon earth.[42]

In his *Defence of the Philosophick Cabbala* More admits that "when you venture beyond the Literal sense, you are not taught by the Scripture, but what you have learned some other way, you apply thereto,"[43] and in the *Defence of the Moral Cabbala* he says he has carefully avoided

> that rock of scandal, that some who are taken for no small Lights in the *Christian* world have cast before

41. Ibid., p. 37.
42. Ibid., pp. 50–51.
43. Ibid., pp. 192, 244.

men, who attenuate all so into Allegories, that they leave the very Fundamentals of Religion suspected, especially themselves not vouchsafing to take notice, that there is any such thing as the *Person of Christ now existent,* much lesse that he is a *Mediatour with God for us,* or that he was a *sacrifice for sin,* when he hung at Jerusalem upon the Crosse.

Many of More's interpretations, however, flatly contradict the historical reality of the Genesis narrative, and it is difficult to see how they may be said to arise naturally from the text even if the narrative is considered fictional. More has thus violated one of the cardinal rules of biblical and indeed all literary interpretation: fidelity to the literal (including the literal-figurative) meaning of the text. In the year 1653 we have come full circle to Origen, the man who, according to Tyndale, started it all.

Milton

In the "spiritual reformers" and in Platonists like Henry More Protestant hermeneutics had come a long way from the forthright position of the early Reformers that *"there is one onely sense, and the same is the literall."*[44] As a poet and theological extremist Milton might be expected to be one of this later company, but as a matter of fact he is not. Both his theory and practice of biblical interpreta-

44. William Perkins, *The Art of Prophecying,* in *Works* (3 vols. Cambridge, 1609), 2, 737.

tion may fairly be described as that of conservative Puritanism.

> No passage of Scripture is to be interpreted in more than one sense; in the Old Testament, however, this sense is sometimes a compound of the historical and typical, as in Hosea xi.1. compared with Matt. ii.15. "out of Egypt have I called my son," which may be explained in a double sense, as referring partly to the people of Israel, and partly to Christ in his infancy.[45]

Nothing could be more orthodox than this formula from the *Christian Doctrine,* unless it is Michael's statement to Adam in *Paradise Lost:*

> So Law appears imperfet, and but giv'n
> With purpose to resign them in full time
> Up to a better Cov'nant, disciplin'd
> From shadowy Types to Truth, from Flesh to Spirit,
> From imposition of strict Laws, to free
> Acceptance of large Grace, from servile fear
> To filial, works of Law to works of Faith.   (XII.300–06)

Most of Milton's references to typology appear in the context of the opposition between the carnal Law and the spiritual Gospel. In *The Reason of Church Government* we read that

---

45. *Christian Doctrine,* I.xxx, *SM,* p. 1040. This is taken from Wollebius. See Maurice Kelley, "Milton's Debt to Wollebius' *Compendium Theologiae Christianae,*" *PMLA, 50* (1935), 158.

In the prophecy of Ezekiel, from the 40th chapter onward, after the destruction of the temple, God, by his prophet, seeking to wean the hearts of the Jews from their old law, to expect a new and more perfect reformation under Christ, sets out before their eyes the stately fabric and constitution of his church, with all the ecclesiastical functions appertaining: indeed the description is, as sorted best to the apprehension of those times, typical and shadowy, but in such manner as never yet came to pass, nor never must literally, unless we mean to annihilate the gospel.[46]

Almost twenty years later in *The Likeliest Means To Remove Hirelings* Milton uses the argument from typology in attacking the system of tithes:

But if it be truer yet, that the priesthood of Aaron typified a better reality, 1 Pet. ii.5, signifying the Christian true and "holy priesthood to offer up spiritual sacrifice;" it follows hence, that we are now justly exempt from paying tithes to any who claim from Aaron, since that priesthood is in us now real, which in him was but a shadow. . . . If Abram, as father of the faithful, paid tithes to Melchisedec, then certainly the ministers also, if they be of that number, paid in him equally with the rest. Which may induce us to believe, that as both Abram and Melchisedec, so tithes also in that action typical and ceremonial,

46. *SM*, p. 508.

signified nothing else but that subjection which all the faithful, both ministers and people, owe to Christ, our high priest and king.[47]

Milton's doctrine of typology may be more precisely located between that of Winstanley and that of orthodox Anglicanism. There is no evidence that Milton denied the historical reality of the Old Testament types, and it is simply irresponsible to charge him with reducing types to a "bundle of metaphors."[48] On the other hand, he rejected utterly the Anglican view that the Old Testament types are fulfilled in the Church and that the physical church and liturgical ceremonies and vestments symbolize the inner life of the Christian. For Milton all the outward, ceremonial aspects of the Old Law by which the bishops justified the practices of the Anglican Church were "beggarly rudiments,"[49] and those who wished to perpetuate them had "judaized the church."[50] "The whole ceremonial law . . . comprehends nothing but the propitiatory office of Christ's priesthood, which being in substance accomplished, both law and priesthood fades away of itself, and passes into air like a transitory vision."[51] "Believe it, wondrous doctors, all corporeal resemblances of inward holiness and beauty are now past; he that will clothe the gospel now, intimates plainly that the gospel is naked, uncomely,

47. Ibid., pp. 882–83.
48. Malcolm M. Ross, *Poetry and Dogma* (New Brunswick, 1954), p. 99.
49. Gal. 4:9, quoted by Milton in *A Treatise of Civil Power, SM*, p. 873.
50. *Likeliest Means To Remove Hirelings, SM*, p. 885.
51. *Reason of Church Government, SM*, pp. 512, 528.

that I may not say reproachful." Priestly vestments do not symbolize inward purity of heart. The vestments of the Old Testament were foreshadowings of the inward purity of Christians and had no symbolic value at all for the Jews, who were content, according to Milton, to remain in the letter of the law. The vestments of the Anglicans are not symbols but merely indications that they have tried to make "God earthly and fleshly, because they could not make themselves heavenly and spiritual."[52]

Milton's belief that under the Law God spoke obscurely through types, shadows, and outward resemblances that were completely abrogated with the coming of Christ has important implications for his later poetry and for the relation between the poems and his religious thought, but these implications cannot all be explored at once. Lest the reader find himself in wandering mazes lost in the chapters that follow, let me present the thread of my argument. Chapter 3 examines Milton's theory of biblical metaphor and figurative language in general in the context of recent discussions of the language of *Paradise Lost,* and it suggests that Milton could hardly have regarded himself as a Moses Anglicus who "accommodated" his ineffable vision to the understanding of ordinary mortals. The first section of Chapter 4 tries to show that in the description of the Garden and the War in Heaven Milton uses the method of Christian typology rather than Neoplatonic allegory, and some ramifications of this topic are

52. *Of Reformation, SM,* p. 441.

explored. The rest of the chapter develops the contrast between Neoplatonic and Christian modes of thought and language by an examination of the traditional doctrine of the ascent of the soul to God by means of meditation on the "book of nature." A particular aspect of this theme, the contemplation of visual beauty as the first step in the "ladder of love," is the subject of the first section of Chapter 5, which then goes on to examine some of the implications for *Paradise Lost* of Milton's conviction that Christianity is primarily a religion of the ear. In all of these chapters on *Paradise Lost* one of my chief concerns is to show that Christ is the symbolizing center of Milton's universe and that the symbolic integrity of the poem is guaranteed by Christ's role as "the image, as it were, by which we see God," and the "word by which we hear him." Finally, Chapter 6 relates *Samson Agonistes* and *Paradise Regained* to some of the themes that have been developed.

3

The Method of Accommodation

Metaphor: Sacred and Profane

Let us begin this discussion of Milton's theory of figurative language with a definition of metaphor that seems entirely adequate. According to W. B. Stanford metaphor is

> the process and result of using a term (X) normally signifying an object or concept (A) in such a context that it must refer to another object or concept (B) which is distinct enough in characteristics from A to ensure that in the composite idea formed by the synthesis of the concepts A and B and now symbolized in the word X, the factors A and B retain their conceptual independence even while they merge in the unity symbolized by X.[1]

The literary critic will want to proceed from such a definition to a discussion of the function of metaphor, as W. K. Wimsatt and Cleanth Brooks do when they say that

> metaphor combines the element of necessity or universality (the prime poetic quality which Aristotle no-

1. *Greek Metaphor: Studies in Theory and Practice* (Oxford, 1936), p. 101, quoted by W. K. Wimsatt, *The Verbal Icon* (New York, 1958), p. 128.

ticed) with that other element of concreteness or spec-
ificity which was implicit in Aristotle's requirement of
the mimetic object. . . . It is only in metaphor, and
hence it is *par excellence* in poetry, that we encounter
the most radically and relevantly fused union of the
detail and the universal idea.[2]

This would seem to be all the conceptual apparatus
needed to carry on a discussion of how metaphor works in
any given poem, but many critics of Milton have not found
it so. The special nature of Milton's subject and the unique
qualities of his language have called forth theories about
his use of metaphor and about the relationship of language
in general to reality that find no support in Renaissance
conceptions of metaphor or in Milton's own theory and
practice. According to Isabel MacCaffrey the paucity of
metaphor in *Paradise Lost* and the nature of the metaphors
that Milton does use may be explained by his choice of a
"mythic subject." Since myth is

> the source rather than the product of history and na-
> ture, the myth is not to be illuminated by analogies
> with historical events and natural objects. A mythic
> event does not stand for anything else; it is what
> everything else stands for. . . . Metaphorical or (broad-
> ly speaking) allegorical styles in which meaning is
> enacted or adumbrated by analogous incidents and
> symbols are therefore inappropriate for a poem that
> finds its subject in myth.

2. *Literary Criticism: A Short History* (New York, 1957), p. 749.

The varieties of metaphorical and allegorical language used by Donne, Shakespeare, and Wordsworth, for example, "to put the point spectacularly, are styles for a fallen world." "When the object is completely seen at once metaphor is unnecessary; it is saturated with the 'meaning' that we usually apply to it from outside."[3]

Being fallen creatures we cannot see objects in this way, but according to Anne Davidson Ferry the inspired poet could, and he has tried to communicate his vision by a mode of expression called "sacred metaphor." *Paradise Lost*, Mrs. Ferry says, uses various kinds of language: the language of statement, in which the inspired narrator makes didactic comments; the language of analogy, "when he uses similes to contrast the world of his own experience with the unfallen world of his poem"; the language of allegory and parody, which is "another means of expressing the contrast between the inspired narrator's unified vision and the divided consciousness of fallen beings";[4] and the language of sacred metaphor, in which the unified vision of the narrator and the real unity of the unfallen world are expressed. Metaphor does not carry for Mrs. Ferry the same implications about the relation of language to reality that it does for Mrs. MacCaffrey. The latter regards it as a "device of rhetoric and dialectic," appropriate to fallen man, which describes an object "by comparing it with something else, joining two universes of discourse."[5]

3. MacCaffrey, Paradise Lost *as "Myth,"* p. 38.
4. *Milton's Epic Voice* (Cambridge, Mass., 1963), pp. 88, 131.
5. MacCaffrey, p. 108.

Mrs. Ferry on the other hand thinks that metaphor is an "unfallen" style, as it were, since it "insists upon unity rather than separation, identity rather than contrast." What she has in mind, however, is a special kind of metaphor, namely the use of a word conveying both a concrete and an abstract meaning at the same time, as in the opening lines of the poem where the word "Fruit" means both the literal fruit of the Tree and the consequences of eating it.[6] Most of Mrs. Ferry's examples, significantly, are taken from the first two books of *Paradise Lost,* and she adduces the well-known distortions of language by which Milton "presents Hell as at once an area and a plight, a physical and a spiritual reality."[7] It might seem curious that the language of sacred metaphor, by which Milton expresses the unity and luminosity of the unfallen world, should be used so extensively with the archetypal fallen world, but Mrs. Ferry's point is that this language expresses the narrator's inspired vision of the divine truth about Hell, a truth that is hidden from the fallan Satan. Thus when Satan says, "The mind is its own place, and in itself / Can make a Heav'n of Hell, a Hell of Heav'n" (I.254–55), he is ignorant of the fact "that our spiritual 'place' and our 'place' in the order of being are identical, are interchangeable terms in a single metaphor."[8] (Mrs. Ferry is apparently unwilling to commit herself to the view that spiritual "place" and physical "place" are identical. In the passage

6. Ferry, pp. 92, 93.
7. Ibid., p. 97.
8. Ibid., p. 98.

just quoted, both of her uses of "place" are metaphorical and thus are not interchangeable terms in a single metaphor. As a matter of fact, in the order of being Satan is an angel, and his "place" in the order of being is not identical with his spiritual "place.") There is no use denying that Satan's vision of reality is distorted because he has cut himself off from the source of truth, but that does not mean that he has an inadequate comprehension of Hell. If he at first makes the mistake of assuming that it is merely a place, he soon learns to think of it in terms of sacred metaphor:

> Which way I fly is Hell; myself am Hell;
> And in the lowest deep a lower deep
> Still threat'ning to devour me opens wide,
> To which the Hell I suffer seems a Heav'n.
>
> (IV.75–78)

Satan is usually a dogged literalist, and his characteristic habit of mind and language is one of reduction. When it comes to interpreting his own experience, however, he can be a symbolist like anyone else—and not only concerning his own experience: of Adam and Eve he can say that they are "Imparadis't in one another's arms" (IV.506). Indeed, the whole notion of sacred metaphor might almost be called a Satanic fallacy, since, as we shall see later, both Adam and Eve are ensnared because they fail to realize that even a sacred metaphor is, when all is said and done, only a metaphor.

If by the language of sacred metaphor Milton was actually trying to recreate "our lost vision of a world now strange, awesome, distant but perfectly distinct,"[9] it is strange that he did not employ it in his account of the Creation. Actually Book VII probably contains more metaphors than any other book in the poem, but since most of them do not work by playing abstract against concrete meanings, they do not qualify as sacred. And yet they are the means by which Raphael, who is presumably qualified to use the sacred language, describes to Adam, who apparently uses such language himself, the unfallen world in all its pristine splendor:

> He scarce had said, when the bare Earth, till then
> Desert and bare, unsightly, unadorn'd,
> Brought forth the tender Grass, whose verdure clad
> Her Universal Face with pleasant green,
> Then Herbs of every leaf, that sudden flow'r'd
> Op'ning thir various colors, and made gay
> Her bosom smelling sweet: and these scarce blown,
> Forth flourish'd thick the clust'ring Vine, forth crept
> The smelling Gourd, up stood the corny Reed
> Embattl'd in her field: and th' humble Shrub,
> And Bush with frizzl'd hair implicit: last
> Rose as in Dance the stately Trees, and spread
> Thir branches hung with copious Fruit: or gemm'd
> Thir Blossoms: with high Woods the Hills were
>   crown'd,
> With tufts the valleys and each fountain side,
> With borders long the Rivers.   (VII.313–28)

9. Ibid., pp. 114–15.

Here is God's plenty of profane metaphors, and they imply an organic universe in which the human and the nonhuman are in harmony. The passage, however, does not support the contention that "Milton's vision of a single interconnected universe meant that, even when he used metaphor and simile, the vehicle could almost without warning shift and become the tenor,"[10] nor does it suggest that there is a sacred language in *Paradise Lost* by which Milton attempts to recreate our lost vision of "a world in which words perfectly identify things, as the names which Adam gave to the animals corresponded to their natures."[11] Milton no doubt believed that Adam's language corresponded to reality in this way, but he himself cannot use this language for obvious reasons, and he makes no attempt to invent an analogous one. On the contrary, the metaphorical language in which the narrator and Christ speak of the Garden, as we shall see in the next chapter, suggests that the "meaning" of the Garden is not inherent in the objects themselves; it can only be applied to them because of the Fall. If there is a language of sacred metaphor, it is preeminently a language of fallen man.

Neither Mrs. MacCaffrey nor Mrs. Ferry suggests that Milton's use of metaphor entails any particular view, on his part, of the nature of reality. The poetic world he has created, they imply, is Neoplatonic, but that does not necessarily mean that Milton accepted the Neoplatonic

10. MacCaffrey, p. 108.
11. Ferry, p. 115.

ontology. Mrs. Ferry, in fact, is at some pains to contrast the "unfallen" language of sacred metaphor to the "fallen" language of simile, allegory, and parody. Thus Satan's inability to recognize Sin, who was conceived in his own mind, is an illustration of his divided consciousness. "This discrepancy between his inner and outer experience is expressed in the form of allegory, because the tendency which characterizes his fallen vision to disjoin physical and spiritual truths has its parallel in the allegorical method, which depends upon the separation of concrete and abstract meanings."[12] Whether or not we agree with these notions of the function of metaphor, simile, and allegory, it seems clear that Mrs. Ferry does not think that Milton, in adapting various kinds of figurative language to his subject, needed any particular metaphysical collateral to borrow a metaphor. Rosemond Tuve, on the other hand, is an avowed Neoplatonist, and she has no doubt about Milton's allegiance. In her view the linguistic Fall occurred sometime in the eighteenth century. Like Dr. Johnson, modern readers regard allegory as "a set of synonymous correspondences" rather than as "continued metaphor," and they disparagingly refer to metaphor itself as "*mere* metaphor."[13] They are willing to accept the statement that "The halcyons [in the *Nativity Ode*] do stand metaphorically, in the common sense of the word also, for peace, as

12. Ibid., p. 132.
13. Rosemond Tuve, *Images and Themes in Five Poems by Milton* (Cambridge, Mass., 1957), pp. 91, n.10; 108. See the important review by A. J. Smith in *RES*, N.S., *10* (1960), 309–11.

the ocean is metaphorically, to many, turbulence mental
and spiritual" only because "they do not therefore have
to assume that anything lies behind such significances except associations based on the observation of behaviour.
The 'real bird' and the 'real ocean' must maintain an existence separable from *any meanings;* these 'we give' them,
whereas they 'have' habits, properties, qualities—such are
the assumptions in the audience to whom the modern
critic speaks of 'metaphor.' "[14] Such were not, according
to Miss Tuve, the assumptions of a medieval or Renaissance audience. George Herbert, for example,

> writes in symbols because he thus sees the world, both
> outside and inside himself; he sees it as a web of
> significances not as a collection of phenomena which
> we may either endow with significance or leave unen-
> dowed. He writes not of events and facts, but of mean-
> ings and values, and he uncovers rather than creates
> these meanings. . . . He not only respects the world of
> meanings thus presented as real, but in turn, like all
> poets, he embodies in metaphor these values he can-
> not say otherwise. . . . . . This perception of all things
> in their metaphorical dimension is the greatest single
> discovery we can make concerning the quality of life
> by reading the poetry of the sixteenth and seventeenth
> centuries. It was far from new then; for these centu-
> ries it was not a discovery but a habit. It is a mode of

14. Tuve, p. 54, n.6.

approach to truth which Western culture has slighted for some centuries, with bitter results.[15]

In her invaluable study of images and themes in Milton's early poems Miss Tuve links this conception of metaphor, allegory, and symbolism to the doctrine of typology, thus joining together what the theologians discussed in the last chapter tried to keep asunder. She points out that in typology, which she calls "strict allegory," the literal-historical reality of the types was insisted upon, and that "in its greatest days, an essential element in the definition of allegory, which rhetoricians call briefly a metaphor continued, was the reality of the first term." In secularized allegory the first term is not a historical Circe or Red Crosse, nor is it a "personality" like Comus or the Lady, "whose realness consists in their being *individuals.*" "The first term's historical and literal reality consists in its being a true account of every man's innumerable encounters with unregenerate natural man as he meets him in himself, every man's potential capacity to wed himself to Una, and his openness to despair." If this, then, is the literal reality of the first term, which corresponds to the type, what is the reality of the second term, which corresponds to the antitype?

Here readers part company according to their philosophical postulates, but there is no doubt of which company Milton belongs in. It has long seemed to me

15. *A Reading of George Herbert* (Chicago, 1952), pp. 103–04.

that profound allegory is written by (hence read sympathetically by) those who can look with the eyes of the mediaeval realist, or the Platonist (we must cover by our term the "Plato" of later men). The deep-dyed nominalist (or positivist) can find no second term. He is left with merely a series of recurrent psychological happenings, which his interpretation of one man's covetousness proliferates when he calls it Covetousness and sees it as resembling all other examples of men being covetous, or which his interpretation of one Lady's rejection of Pleasure's Cup proliferates when he sees it as like all other such refusals. For Sidney, as for Spenser's greater figures, we must take out that last *like*. Both, like those I have opposed to the nominalist, would find a metaphorical identity in the refusals by virtue of their being significant of a second term real in another sense than they. The reality which Una and the Lady (and any of us who can) make manifest, which the dark offers of Comus and Despair and our own betraying minds "present", has its being as the "forms" of things have being for Sidney, as the ideas have being for Spenser. The simultaneous presentation of the two modes of reality is the real excitement of allegory.[16]

Marjorie Nicholson also ascribes a special use of metaphor to Renaissance writers, though she has her eye on the sensible realm rather than the supersensible:

16. Tuve, pp. 158–59.

64

"Modern cosmology, like its predecessors, is based on an analogy." But we are aware that it *is* an analogy. We know that we are attempting to explain the universe and the world and man by figures of speech deliberately drawn from history, on the one hand, and natural science on the other. We think of our universe in similes. Our Elizabethan ancestors thought of their world in metaphors. The world was not *like* an animal; it *was* animate.[17]

Miss Nicholson need not have hedged by choosing the adjective "animate," since there were at least some Renaissance writers who thought that the world was literally an "animal."[18] Unfortunately, it is impossible to identify them by their use of metaphor. Take the following lines, for example:

As the drie ground that thirstes after a showr
Seemes to rejoyce when it is well iwet,
And speedely brings foorth both grasse and flowr,
If lacke of sunne or season doo not let.

The author of these lines may have thought that the world was animate, but Puttenham did not. Here is his comment:

Here for want of an apter and more naturall word to declare the drie temper of the earth, it is said to thirst

17. *The Breaking of the Circle* (Evanston, 1950), p. xix. The first sentence is quoted from R. G. Collingwood, *The Idea of Nature*.

18. The whole world "is one Creature by it self, and one animall, and lives like an animall, having in it self its vitall spirit" (Valentine Weigelius, *ASTROLOGIE Theologized* [London, 1649], p. 32).

and to rejoyce, which is onely proper to living creatures, and yet being so inverted, doth not so much
swerve from the true sence, but that every man can
easilie conceive the meaning thereof.[19]

Thomas Wilson, who also lived some years before "Baco-
nian common sense triumphed over mysticism,"[20] reveals a
similar "modern" tendency to regard metaphor as
grounded in similitude: "A *Metaphore* is an alteration of
a worde, from the proper and naturall meaning, to that
which is not proper, and yet agreeth thereunto by some
likenesse, that appereth to be in it." One of his categories
includes "translations" from the living to the nonliving:
"From the living to the not living, wee use many translations. As thus. You shall pray for all men, dispersed
throughout the face of the earth. The arme of a Tree. The
side of a bancke. The land crieth for vengeaunce."[21] There
is nothing in Renaissance rhetorical theory to suggest that
the use of metaphor implies one view of reality rather than
another, and there is nothing in Renaissance poetic practice to suggest that only a medieval realist or a Platonist
can write a metaphoric, symbolic, or profoundly allegorical work. Whatever the philosophical allegiance of poets
like Sidney and Spenser, Milton was anything but a Neo-

19. *The Arte of English Poesie,* ed. Gladys Willcock and Alice Walker
(Cambridge, Cambridge University Press, 1936), p. 179.

20. Nicholson, p. xxii.

21. *The arte of Rhetorique* 1560, ed. G. H. Mair (Oxford, Clarendon
Press, 1909), p. 173.

platonist, as I try to show in the chapters that follow, and he is one of the company of mundane rhetoricians when he defines metaphor as "a similitude contracted to one word without signs, which, however, are understood."[22] It may well be that Milton would have regarded as non-metaphorical certain expressions that nominalists and positivists regard as "mere metaphors," but there are probably fewer of them than we think, and in any case there is no a priori way of identifying them. Since Milton did not write a handbook of rhetoric, we do not know what he thought of the examples just quoted from Puttenham and Wilson. Fortunately, however, there are enough scattered references in his prose works both early and late to enable us to get a pretty clear idea of what he thought the function of metaphor was.[23]

Our first example may be prefaced by a quotation from Mrs. Ferry:

> Adam and Eve before the Fall repeatedly use the language of Genesis to describe their union. Their reiterated references to the creation of Eve from Adam's side, their sense of unity in "flesh" and "bone," as one being, "parts" of one "soul," insist upon the simultaneous truth of the story as concrete, historical fact and

22. *Art of Logic,* I.21, in *The Works of John Milton,* ed. Frank Allen Patterson and others (18 vols. in 21, New York, Columbia University Press, 1933), *11,* 197.

23. The reader is again referred to the excellent article by H. R. MacCallum, "Milton and Figurative Interpretation of the Bible."

as abstract, spiritual reality. The diction provided by Genesis refers to both meanings simultaneously.[24]

Whatever Milton the inspired narrator of *Paradise Lost* may have thought, Milton the prose pamphleteer did not think the biblical statement that man and wife are "one flesh" was anything more than an everyday metaphor. In *Colasterion,* answering the argument of his adversary that a husband "may not divorce for any disagreement no more than he may separate his soul from his body," Milton says "that to divorce a relative and metaphorical union of two bodies into one flesh cannot be likened in all things to the dividing of that natural union of soul and body into one person, is apparent of itself."[25] Here Milton is not talking about Adam and Eve, of course, but even in *Paradise Lost* one of Adam's mistakes is precisely that he thinks in terms of sacred metaphor. That is, he interprets the expression "one flesh" (or rather, he interprets the actual fact that Eve was created from one of his ribs) as guaranteeing the "spiritual reality" of their oneness:

> Flesh of Flesh,
> Bone of my Bone thou art, and from thy State
> Mine never shall be parted, bliss or woe.
>
> (IX.914–16)

> Our State cannot be sever'd, we are one,
> One Flesh; to lose thee were to lose myself.
>
> (IX.958–59)

24. Ferry, *Milton's Epic Voice*, p. 117.
25. *SM*, p. 716.

Misinterpreting the metaphor, Adam does not realize that he and Eve are literally two and only metaphorically one so long as they are united in love of God and obedience to Him. When Eve sins, they are no longer metaphorically one. Had Adam realized this, he might have tried to re-unite her will to his and to God's instead of justifying his own sin by appealing to their physical union.

More conclusive evidence of the way Milton interpreted metaphors may be found in his doctrine of the sacraments, for a Christian's sacramental theory defines the limit to which he is willing to push his theory of metaphorical and symbolic expression. If a person believes that the sacraments, defined as visible signs instituted by God, are analogies or similitudes which represent rather than present a spiritual reality, he will surely accord no higher status to man-made signs. This is precisely what Milton believed. Speaking of the Lord's Supper he says,

> That *living bread* therefore which Christ calls *his flesh,* and that *blood* which is *drink indeed,* can be nothing but the doctrine of Christ's having become man in order to shed his blood for us; a doctrine which whosoever receives by faith shall as surely attain eternal life, as the partaking of meats and drinks supports our brief term of bodily existence.[26]

In speaking of the sacraments, Milton says, the sacred writers frequently employed a figure "by which whatever

26. *Christian Doctrine,* I.xxviii, *SM,* p. 1033.

illustrates or signifies any particular thing is used to denote, not what it is in itself, but what it illustrates or signifies." Thus circumcision is called "a covenant," and a lamb is called "the passover." "The object of the sacred writers, in thus expressing themselves," he continues, "was probably to denote the close affinity between the sign and the thing signified, as well as, by a bold metaphor, to intimate the certainty with which the seal is thus set to spiritual blessings."[27] In the sacraments of the Old Testament the "close affinity between the sign and the thing signified" results from a particular command of God or a particular historical event and not from any "meaning" that might be inherent in the objects themselves. In the sacraments of the New Testament there is no doubt a more "natural" affinity, and a constant theme of Protestant devotional writings is "the use of the sacraments . . . to help our souls by our senses."[28] But this is a theme that appears nowhere in Milton, so strong is his torque, at least in his religion, away from the material and toward the spiritual, away (one might say) from the vehicle and toward the tenor.

Elsewhere in the *Christian Doctrine* Milton evidences the same cautious, rationalistic approach to metaphor that Bacon, Hobbes, and the proponents of the Royal Society do. In the chapter on predestination he says, "Again, if an argument of any weight in the discussion of so contro-

27. Ibid.
28. Richard Sibbes, *The Soul's Conflict with Itself* (1635), ed. A. B. Grosart in *Works*, Nichol's Standard Divines (6 vols. Edinburgh, 1863), *1*, 185.

verted a subject can be derived from allegorical and metaphorical expressions, mention is frequently made of those
who are written among the living, and of the book of life,
but never of the book of death." Later in the same chapter
he says that God's reply to Moses in Exodus 32.32,33, "although metaphorical, explains with sufficient clearness
that the principle of predestination depends upon a condition—'whosoever hath sinned, him will I blot out.' "[29]
Like metaphors, figurative language in general is to be
interpreted in the light of nonfigurative statements and
the analogy of faith. In *The Tenure of Kings and Magistrates* Milton says that "the pathetical words of a psalm can
be no certain decision to a point that hath abundantly
more certain rules to go by,"[30] and in *A Treatise of Civil
Power* he says that a parable is not to be "strained through
every word or phrase":

> Yet some are so eager in their zeal of forcing, that
> they refuse not to descend at length to the utmost
> shift of that parabolical proof, Luke xiv. 16, &c.,
> "Compel them to come in:" therefore magistrates may
> compel in religion. As if a parable were to be strained
> through every word or phrase, and not expounded by
> the general scope thereof; which is no other here than
> the earnest expression of God's displeasure on those
> recusant Jews, and his purpose to prefer the Gentiles
> on any terms before them: expresssed here by the

29. I.iv, *SM,* pp. 931, 934.
30. *SM,* p. 758.

word compel. But how compels he? Doubtless no other wise than he draws, without which no man can come to him, John v. 44; and that is by the inward persuasive motions of his Spirit, and by his ministers; not by the outward compulsions of a magistrate or his officers.[31]

The suggestion that the greatest poet of the age shares a distrust of metaphor with the odious Thomas Hobbes will come as a shock only to those who still think that the famous "attack on metaphor" was an attack on poetry, which (taken by itself) it was not, since it was concerned with the use of metaphor not in poetry but in rational prose discourse. Bacon was neither the first nor the last to suggest that metaphors may serve to darken counsel, and one need not be embarrassed at finding Milton in this company.

Milton did not, however, go as far as the Cambridge Platonist John Smith did when he cited with approval Plutarch's statement that

> God hath now taken away from his Oracles Poetrie, and the variety of dialect, and circumlocution, and obscuritie; and hath so ordered them to speak to those that consult them, as the Laws doe to the Cities under their subjection, and Kings to their people, and Masters to their Scholars, in the most intelligible and perswasive language.[32]

31. Ibid., pp. 872–73.
32. *Select Discourses* (London, 1660), pp. 264–65.

Milton makes one exception to his general rule of interpretation: biblical language about God is in a class by itself.

> Our safest way [of knowing God] is to form in our minds such a conception of God, as shall correspond with his own delineation and representation of himself in the sacred writings. For granting that both in the literal and figurative descriptions of God, he is exhibited not as he really is, but in such a manner as may be within the scope of our comprehension, yet we ought to entertain such a conception of him, as he, in condescending to accommodate himself to our capacities, has shown that he desires we should conceive. . . .
>
> There is no need then that theologians should have recourse here to what they call anthropopathy—a figure invented by the grammarians to excuse the absurdities of the poets on the subject of the heathen divinities. . . .
>
> Let us be convinced that those have acquired the truest apprehension of the nature of God who submit their understandings to his word; considering that he has accommodated his word to their understandings, and has shown what he wishes their notion of the Deity should be. . . .
>
> In arguing thus, we do not say that God is in fashion like unto man in all his parts and members, but that as far as we are concerned to know, he is of that form

which he attributes to himself in the sacred writings.[33]

Here and here only Milton refuses to conceptualize the figurative language of the Bible, and in this respect (it may be added) he is almost alone among his Protestant contemporaries. In interpreting biblical passages that do not refer to God Himself, however, Milton consistently distrusts metaphorical statements of doctrine and seeks to go behind them by referring to other, literal statements, even in passages referring to Christ and the sacraments. It is therefore difficult to understand what it means to say that Milton uses the *method* of accommodation in *Paradise Lost,* since he would hardly arrogate to himself a mode of understanding and expression that he denies to the human authors of the Bible and reserves to God alone. He of course uses the biblical *language* by which God has accommodated Himself to our understandings, but this does not make him a Moses who has "looked on the face of truth unveiled." Nor does the fact that Raphael, as a fictional character, tells Adam that he must use the method of accommodation in describing the War in Heaven mean that Milton thought that he himself was in possession of truths so ineffable that he had to "accommodate" them to ordinary human understanding by veiling them in myth and allegory. As a fictional character the narrator does indeed lay claim to such knowledge, but unless we are willing to grant that John Milton was literally inspired, there seems

33. *Christian Doctrine,* I.ii, *SM,* pp. 923–24.

to be no meaningful way to relate this fictional claim to the language of *Paradise Lost*.

Lively Image

There is, however, quite another theory of accommodation that is entirely relevant to what Milton is doing in *Paradise Lost*. In this theory the words "accommodation" and "accommodative" refer not to a mode of expression but to a mode of interpreting the Bible for homiletic purposes. As we saw in the last chapter, both Catholic and Protestant theologians recognized that many biblical passages may be applied homiletically in a sense not intended by the author in order to illustrate or bring home to the listener some point of doctrine or morals. Indeed, this was the back door by which many Catholic spiritual "meanings" found their way into Protestant sermons and devotional writings. In this homiletic context the word "accommodation" implies exactly the reverse of what it does in the humanist and Neoplatonist theory that divine poets like Moses and Orpheus veil arcane truths in poetic allegories because they cannot be communicated in any other way or because they would otherwise be profaned by the vulgar—a theory, incidentally, that the youthful Milton appears to endorse in his Prolusion on the music of the spheres, though it is impossible to know what degree of assent he accorded it. To bring the discussion back to typology, we observe that some Catholic theologians spoke of the types and the spiritual sense in general in this way.

75

Protestants, on the other hand, contrasted the veils and shadows of the Old Testament with the full light of the New, as in the following passages:

> For all that were before Christ were in the infancy and childhood of the world; and saw that sun which we see openly, but through a cloud, and had but feeble and weak imaginations of Christ, as children have of men's deeds, a few prophets except, which yet described him unto other in sacrifices and ceremonies, likenesses, riddles, proverbs, and dark and strange speaking, until the full age were come, that God would shew him openly unto the whole world, and deliver them from their shadows and cloud-light, and the heathen out of their dead sleep of stark blind ignorance.

> The Apostle [in Heb. 10:1] then puts this difference betweene the law and the Gospell: to wit, that that which at this day is drawne and painted with fresh and lively colours, was onely shadowed out under the law by a rude or grosse draught.

> As in the Creation darknes went before light, or as the dawning precedes the brightnesse of the day, & as Joseph obscurely at first behaved himselfe unto his Brethren, and Moses covered with a vaile stood before the people: Even so (Right Reverend) in the detection of the glorious worke of mans Redemption, mysticall promises went before mercifull perfor-

mance, darke shaddowes were the fore-runners of
that bright substance, obscure types were harbingers
to that glorious Anti-type the Messiah.[34]

Before the advent of Christ God did indeed veil His sav-
ing truths in shadowy types and ceremonies, but for Christians, who live in the full light of the Gospel, the purpose
of types is not to veil but to illuminate and make "lively"
the truths that are already known. Their function, in
short, is rhetorical and may be regarded as analogous to
the function of figurative language in general.

Flacius Illyricus makes this analogy between types and
figures of speech explicit when he says that many Old
Testament ceremonies are obscure allegories, as does
Nathaniel Ingelo when, putting the comparison another
way, he says that parables are "lively images of usefull
Truths . . . and they do, as the Epistle to the Hebrews
saith of *Moses* his shadows, by way of type and resemblance they do minister to the knowledge of heavenly
matters."[35] The most explicit analogy of all is drawn by
Tyndale when he says that although we can prove nothing
with Old Testament ceremonies,

yet when we have once found out Christ and his
mysteries, then we may borrow figures, that is to say

34. Tyndale, *A Prologue into . . . Leviticus,* in *Works, 1,* 27; Calvin, *A
Commentarie on the Whole Epistle to the Hebrewes* (London, 1605), p. 201;
William Guild, *MOSES UNVAILED* (London, 1620), Epistle Dedicatorie.
35. Flacius, *Clavis,* col. 68; Ingelo, *The Perfection, Authority, and Credi-
bility of the Holy Scriptures* (London, 1659), pp. 1-2.

allegories, similitudes, or examples to open Christ, and the secrets of God hid in Christ, even unto the quick, and to declare them more lively and sensibly with them than with all the words of the world. For similitudes have more virtue and power with them than bare words, and lead a man's wits farther into the pith and marrow and spiritual understanding of the thing than all the words that can be imagined.[36]

It is perhaps significant that two key words which appear with great frequency in discussions of typology, "shadow" and "lively," also appear in literary discussions of figures of speech. The word "shadow," which usually means type in a religious context, is frequently used by Renaissance poets and critics to mean allegory or symbol, as when Thomas Lodge says that in the *Aeneid* "under the shadow of byrds, beastes, and trees the follies of the world were disiphered," or when Gascoigne says that if he were to disclose his "pretense in love," he would discover his "disquiet in shadowes *per Allegoriam.*"[37] For literary examples of the use of "lively" we need go only to Puttenham, who says that our learned forefathers set down six rules for good utterance, the sixth of which was that "it should be lively & stirring, which they called Tropus," and to Bacon, who says that "the Fable and fiction of *Scylla* seemeth to be a lively Image" of Scholastic philoso-

36. Tyndale, *A Prologue into . . . Leviticus*, p. 28.
37. Lodge, *Defence of Poetry*, in *Elizabethan Critical Essays*, ed. G. G. Smith (London, 1904), *1*, 65; Gascoigne, *Certayne Notes of Instruction*, ibid., 48.

phy. To set beside this quotation from Bacon there is Calvin's statement that the house of Abraham is "a lively image of Gods Churche."[38]

The rhetorical function of allegory and figurative language in general was a commonplace of Protestant homiletic theory and practice, and the example of the Bible provided whatever justification was felt to be needed.

> The putting of lively colours upon common truths hath oft a strong working both upon the fancy and our will and affections . . . our Saviour Christ's manner of teaching was by a lively representation to men's fancies, to teach them heavenly truths in an earthly, sensible manner.[39]

According to Tyndale "a similitude, or an ensample, doth print a thing much deeper in the wits of a man, than doth

---

38. *The Arte of English Poetry*, III.viii, ibid., 2, 162; *The Advancement of Learning*, ed. William Aldis Wright (Oxford, Clarendon Press, 1868), p. 33; *Sermons of M. John Calvine upon the Epistle of Saincte Paule to the Galathians* (London, 1574), p. 215v.

39. Sibbes, *The Soul's Conflict with Itself*, in *Works, 1*, 184–85. U. Milo Kaufmann, in *The Pilgrim's Progress and Traditions in Puritan Meditation* (New Haven, 1966), an excellent book that I was unable to see before my manuscript was completed, places Sibbes in a wider context of Puritan meditation than my own knowledge enabled me to provide. He suggests that Sibbes provided "what is perhaps the first important consolidation of insights native to the tradition of heavenly meditation that are relevant to Bunyan's use of the imagination" (p. 145). According to Kaufmann the earlier tradition of Puritan meditation, which (curiously) seems to stem from the Anglican Joseph Hall, was hostile to the "imagination." See the whole of Chapter 6.

a plain speaking, and leaving behind him as it were a sting to prick him forward, and to awake him withal," and Bullinger speaks to the same effect when he says that "men do more easily conceive and understand the doctrine of heavenly things, when it is shadowed out under some dark and covert sign of earthly things, than when it is nakedly and spiritually indeed delivered."[40] Many sixteenth- and seventeenth-century Protestants (though not Milton) speak of the sacramental elements in the same way. "Whilst the soul is joined with the body," says Richard Sibbes, "it hath not only a necessary but a holy use of imagination, and of sensible things whereupon our Imagination worketh. What is the use of the sacraments but to help our souls by our senses, and our faith by imagination?" Thomas Becon says that the sacraments "are testimonies, signs, and seals of God's grace, favour, and mercy toward us, and do lively represent and set forth unto us the great clemency and singular goodness of God toward all such as repent . . . and in fine . . . the sacraments are the very same to the believing Christian, that 'the word of God is,' as St Austin saith: 'A sacrament is a visible word.' " Finally, Dudley Fenner says that the difference between the Passover and the Lord's Supper is "that in the worde and by the worde alone our faith is wrought, wee truely receyve Christe by faith," but they are similar in that "in these Sacraments our faith is quickened, confirmed, and increased, & so

40. Tyndale, *The Obedience of a Christian Man*, in *Works, 1*, 342; Henry Bullinger, *Decades* (Cambridge, Parker Society, 1852), p. 243 (Decade 5, Sermon 6).

doeth more fullie, livelie, and comfortablie applie Christ and his benefites."[41]

If we view *Paradise Lost* in the context of biblical interpretation and Christian homiletics that has been presented in the last two chapters, we will probably be inclined to think that Milton regarded himself as more nearly a preacher than a Moses Anglicus or an Orphic poet, especially when we recall his statement that the abilities of the poet "are of power beside the office of a pulpit, to inbreed and cherish in a great people the seeds of virtue and public civility, to allay the perturbations of the mind and set the affections in right tune."[42] Poetry and rhetoric were closely allied in Renaissance theory,[43] and Milton himself defined poetry as differing in degree rather than in kind from rhetoric, being "more simple, sensuous, and passionate." He might well have applied to *Paradise Lost* Richard Baxter's description of his own preaching: "For that is the main work that I drive at through all; That you may not stick in a bare Thinking, but may have the lively sense of all upon your *hearts*."[44] Milton is a Christian poet who lives in the full light of the Gospel day, not a prophet under the old dispensation of types and shadows, and his

---

41. Sibbes, *Works, 1*, 185; *The Early Works of Thomas Becon* (Cambridge, Parker Society, 1843), p. 12; Fenner, *The Whole Doctrine of the Sacraments* (Middleburg, 1588), Sig. B5r and v.

42. *Reason of Church Government, SM*, p. 525.

43. K. G. Hamilton, *The Two Harmonies* (Oxford, Clarendon Press, 1963), Chap. 2. See also the trenchant remarks of Rosemond Tuve, "A Name To Resound for Ages," *The Listener, 60* (28 Aug. 1958), 312–13.

44. *The Saints Everlasting Rest* (London, 1650), p. 216.

function is to create "lively images" of the truths that are available to every faithful Christian. Like the preachers who defended the "putting of lively colours upon common truths"[45] by appealing to the example of the Bible, Milton turned to the Bible not only as the source of Christian truth but also as a model of expression. *Paradise Lost* is a fiction (in which certain historical events are narrated and "allegorically accommodated") that is analogous to the Bible not in its structure but in its modes of discourse. It contains literal narrative (most of which Milton could hardly have regarded as anything but fictional); literal statements of doctrine; prophecy; vision; psalms; types (as we shall see later Milton creates his own types out of the narrative: they are thus analogous to and not identical with the authentic Old Testament types, to which he merely refers); "accommodations" to limited understanding (Raphael's narration of the War in Heaven to Adam); and allegory, similitudes, metaphors, and other kinds of figurative language. If we interpret *Paradise Lost* by the rules of biblical interpretation commonly accepted by Milton and his Protestant contemporaries, if we understand figurative expressions in the light of clear, literal statements, if we interpret obscure passages by the "analogy of faith" as it were, if we do not strain Milton's parable "through every word or phrase," we shall perhaps be spared the excesses associated with the modern counterparts of the "crabbed textuists"[46] on the one hand and the "monkish" allegorizers on the other. In saying this I do not mean

45. Sibbes, *Works, 1,* 184.
46. *The Doctrine and Discipline of Divorce, SM,* p. 577.

to imply that we should read *Paradise Lost* as we read the *Christian Doctrine*. On the contrary, the next two chapters will bring a good deal of pressure to bear on certain key images and words. I am convinced, however, that the integrity of *Paradise Lost* is violated if the figurative statements are isolated from the nonfigurative ones, and I suggest that the poem's organic unity may best be preserved by viewing Milton's images not only in the immediate context of the poem but also in the larger literary and theological context from which Milton drew them. Not everyone will want to read *Paradise Lost* in this way, and I have no quarrel with these readers so long as they do not attribute to Milton their own views of the nature of language and its relation to thought and reality.

The burden of the next two chapters will be to prove that it is more meaningful to describe the symbolic method of *Paradise Lost* as Christian than as Platonic or Neoplatonic. Indeed, I hope to show that the poem may be described in some respects as anti-Neoplatonic, not only in its symbolic method but also in its central thematic concerns. Milton charges the key Neoplatonic symbols with Christian significance and thus reverses their polarity, as it were, and in this activity the role of Christ is central. If it is true, as Louis Martz brilliantly pleads,[47] that the Garden is the symbolic center of the poem in the sense that from it the chief metaphors of the spiritual life are drawn, it is also true that Christ is the symbolizing center of the poem since it is through Him that the poem's major metaphors find their significance. In the *Christian Doctrine* Milton

47. *The Paradise Within* (New Haven, 1964), esp. pp. 105–67.

says that "the Word is both Son and Christ, that is, as I say, *anointed;* and as he is the image, as it were, by which we see God, so is he the word by which we hear him."[48] Not only is Christ as Word of God the symbolizing center, but Christ as Image of God radiates from the literal center of *Paradise Lost.* His role as Judge of the rebel angels at the end of Book VI, which is a foreshadowing of his role at the Last Judgment, is assumed again in Book X when he judges Adam, and his role as Creator at the beginning of Book VII is anticipated in Book III, where he is revealed as man's intercessor and re-creator. In Book IV the Garden is a fleshly type of the future "Paradise within," which is the image of Christ in man, and in Book IX occurs the event which destroys that Garden and makes the metaphoric transformation possible, with the literalist Satan enacting the role of a false Christ through his "foul descent" and his promise of godhead by eating the literal Fruit. In Book V the Father metaphorically "begets" (i.e. exalts) his Son, and in Book VIII Adam literally begets Eve and exalts her above all Creation, with the result that it is her voice he hears rather than God's (X.145–46). The absence of Christ in the fallen world of the devils in Books I and II is the most terrifying example of His justice, and in Books XI and XII His presence in human history is the most glorious example of His mercy. *Paradise Lost* thus illustrates the cardinal rule of biblical interpretation: the whole Bible speaks of Christ. He is the lively image foreshadowed in the types of the Old Testament and fully revealed in the truth of the New.

48. *Christian Doctrine,* I.vi, *SM,* p. 973.

4

Neoplatonic and Christian Symbols
in *Paradise Lost*

Paradise Lost brings into dramatic and symbolic confrontation two modes of thought that appear in varying proportions in the Christian tradition. On the one hand there is the Greek, and especially the Platonic and Neoplatonic, emphasis on ontology, on the universe as a harmonious and proportioned structure, on the regularity of nature as the visible manifestation of the logos that is immanent in the world; on the other hand there is the Hebrew emphasis on psychology, on the primacy of individual encounters with God and of particular covenants with Him, and on nature as the setting in which these encounters take place. In Greek thought the emphasis is on the present, the Eternal Now which bodies forth the rational structure of the universe. In Hebrew thought the emphasis is on history as the embodiment of God's purpose, and history is especially the record of those specific times when God communicated with man in a special way. The past and the future thus assume an importance they do not have in classicism.

Christianity has tried to embrace, not always with success, both of these intuitions. In general it may be said that the Middle Ages leaned toward the Greek view: the daily monastic office, the daily celebration of the sacred liturgy, the sacramental system, the systematization of theology, the philosophical interest in being rather than becoming, the emphasis on the visual rather than the auditory, the elaborate system of static correspondences between the earthly and the heavenly, all bespeak a primary (though of course not exclusive) interest in the timeless structure of eternity as physically manifested in the natural world and in the forms and symbols of daily life. The Reformation, on the other hand, leans to the Hebrew view: history, both corporate and individual, assumes more importance, and the idea of personal encounter with God and of a covenant with Him replaces the idea of a daily reenactment of the eternal Incarnation. The physical church is no longer the scene in which the eternal drama is presented; it is the actual meeting place where men come together to hear the Word of God.[1]

In *Paradise Lost* Milton subjects the symbolic system of Neoplatonism to the same searching scrutiny that he directs at classical ideals of heroism and at other classical systems of ethics and cosmology.[2] By embodying epic heroism in the person of Satan, and various other classical

1. The preceding two paragraphs are heavily indebted to F. W. Dillistone, *Christianity and Symbolism* (Philadelphia, 1955), pp. 44–69.

2. C. M. Bowra, *From Virgil to Milton* (London, 1945); Davis P. Harding, *The Club of Hercules* (Urbana, 1962); William G. Madsen, *The Idea of Nature in Milton's Poetry*, in *Three Studies in the Renaissance* (New Haven, 1958).

ethical systems in the persons of other fallen angels, Milton suggests their antipathy to Christianity. Mindful of Neoplatonism's historic role in the development of Christian theology, he is more gentle toward it, selecting the archangel Raphael as its spokesman. But everything Raphael says about the symbolic correspondences between Heaven and earth, the ascent of the soul, and the ladder of love (familiar Neoplatonic themes that will be discussed in the next two chapters) is undercut by the fact that he is speaking of unfallen man in an unfallen world. He represents, as it were, the highest reach of the pagan intellect, ignorant of "how man fell / Degraded by himself, on grace depending" *(PR,* IV.311–12).

Earth the Shadow of Heaven

what surmounts the reach
Of human sense, I shall delineate so,
By lik'ning spiritual to corporal forms,
As may express them best, though what if Earth
Be but the shadow of Heav'n, and things therein
Each to other like, more than on Earth is thought?

(V.571–76)

In prefacing his account of the War in Heaven with these words, Raphael seems to say that it will not be allegorical or merely metaphorical, but analogical; that although he will have to use the language of accommodation in order to convey his meaning at all, there still may be (he puts the statement in a subordinate clause and in the inter-

87

rogative mood) a relationship between earth and Heaven, between the physical and the spiritual, which is inherent in the nature of things. After Raphael finishes his narrative, however, Adam denies that earth is the shadow of Heaven:

> Great things, and full of wonder in our ears,
> Far differing from this World, thou hast reveal'd
> Divine Interpreter. (VII.70–72)

Adam is right. There is nothing whatever in the world as he knew it that is like the War in Heaven. What did Raphael mean then when he said that earth may be the shadow of Heaven?

Recent commentators without exception have interpreted this phrase in a Neoplatonic sense. "Though the conception of earth as the shadow of heaven has been traced to various sources," says Hughes, "it stems from Plato's doctrine of the universe as formed on a divine and eternal model, and from Cicero's interpretation of it (in *Timaeus ex Platone* ii, 39–41) as implying that 'the world which we see is a simulacrum of an eternal one.' "[3] It is my contention that this interpretation is mistaken, that Milton is using "shadow" here not in its Platonic or Neoplatonic

---

3. *John Milton: Complete Poems and Major Prose* (New York, 1957), p. 315. The Neoplatonic interpretation of Raphael's lines appears also in Hanford, *A Milton Handbook*, p. 205, and in his edition of the poetry; in M. M. Mahood, *Poetry and Humanism* (New Haven, 1950), p. 204; in Paul Shorey, *Platonism Ancient and Modern* (Berkeley, 1938), pp. 41–42, 184; and in all the annotated modern editions of *Paradise Lost* published before 1962 that I have seen.

sense but in its familiar Christian sense of "foreshadow-ing" or "adumbration," and that the symbolism of *Paradise Lost* is typological rather than Platonic.

As Hughes' quotation from Cicero suggests, it is mainly to the *Timaeus* that Plato's followers owe the conception of the visible world as an image, reflection, likeness, or shadow of an eternal world, but the word "shadow" itself is not used in this dialogue. In the *Republic*, however, "shadow" is a key word in the well-known analogies of the Line and the Cave. In trying to explain to his listeners how the philosopher must rise above even a knowledge of virtues like justice and temperance to a knowledge of the good, Socrates asks them to imagine a line divided into two parts, with each of the parts further subdivided. The two main divisions of the line correspond to the visible realm and to the intelligible, and the subdivisions in each main division are compared in respect to their clearness and lack of clearness. The lower subdivision of the visible consists of images *(eikonas)*. "And by images I mean, in the first place, shadows [*skias*], and in the second place, reflections in water and in solid, smooth and polished bodies and the like" (510 A). The higher subdivision of the visible comprises the actual things—animals, artifacts, and so on —of which these are the images or shadows. Corresponding to these two classes of objects are two faculties of the mind; the lower is *eikasia*, or "perception of shadows," and the higher is *pistis*, usually translated "faith" or "conviction." The two subdivisions of the intelligible are related analogously. Corresponding to shadows in the visible realm

89

is the realm of mathematical entities, and corresponding to the faculty of *eikasia* is *dianoia*, "understanding." Corresponding to the higher realm of the visible is the realm of the *archai,* or Forms, which are apprehended by *noēsis,* "reason." Although Plato does say that sense objects are copies or images of Forms, the main point of the analogy of the Line is to distinguish between *dianoia* and *noēsis,* and the distinction between shadows and physical objects is introduced primarily by way of illustration.

In the allegory of the Cave immediately following, Socrates suggests a more graphic analogy of the same relationship. Imagine, he says, a cave in which human beings have been living all their lives facing the back wall, their heads chained so that they cannot turn around. Behind them is a parapet, and behind and above the parapet is a fire. Some men are walking behind the parapet, holding above it statues and figures of animals made of wood, stone, and other materials. The fire casts shadows *(skias)* of these statues on the wall of the cave, which are all these human beings have ever seen and which of course to them are reality. Now suppose, he continues, that one of the prisoners is dragged out of the cave into the sunlight. He would at first be dazzled by the light. Gradually his eyes would grow accustomed to it, first looking on shadows *(skias)* and reflections of things in the water, then at the things themselves, then at the moon and stars at night, and finally at the sun itself, which to Socrates symbolizes the Good. Socrates goes on to explain that in the allegory the cave is the world of sight, the fire is the light of the physical sun, and the journey out of the cave is "the ascent of the soul into the intellectual world" (517 B).

In the *Timaeus,* then, we have the conception of the visible or sensible world as a copy or image of the invisible or intelligible; in the *Republic* the term "shadow" is applied analogously to the things of the sensible world. In the current of thought in late antiquity loosely referred to as Neoplatonism, the conception of the *Timaeus* and the term "shadow" from the *Republic* are fused, as in the following passage from Plotinus:

> He that has the strength, let him arise and withdraw into himself, foregoing all that is known by the eyes, turning away for ever from the material beauty that once made his joy. When he perceives those shapes of grace that show in body, let him not pursue: he must know them for copies, vestiges, shadows, and hasten away toward That they tell of. For if anyone follow what is like a beautiful shape playing over water—is there not a myth telling in symbol of such a dupe, how he sank into the depths of the current and was swept away to nothingness? So too, one that is held by material beauty and will not break free shall be precipitated, not in body but in Soul, down to the dark depths loathed of the Intellective-Being, where, blind even in the Lower-World, he shall have commerce only with shadows, there as here.[4]

4. *Enneads,* I.6.8. Citations from Plotinus in my text are to *The Enneads,* trans. Stephen MacKenna (2d ed. rev. by B. S. Page, London, Faber and Faber Ltd., 1956).

These are metaphors in Plotinus, doubtless, like his comparison of God to light, to which the metaphor of shadow is obviously related. With the Gnostics, however, we are not sure what is metaphor and what is literal statement, at least if Irenaeus is to be trusted. Whatever may have been the intention of the Gnostics themselves when they said that this world was but an image and shadow of the world above, Irenaeus chose to take them literally:

> If, again, they declare that these things [below] are a shadow of those [above], as some of them are bold enough to maintain, so that in this respect they are images, then it will be necessary for them to allow that those things which are above are possessed of bodies. For those bodies which are above do cast a shadow, but spiritual substances do not, since they can in no degree darken others. . . . If, however, they maintain that the shadow spoken of does not exist as being produced by the shade of [those above], but simply in this respect, that [the things below] are far separated from those [above], they will then charge the light of their Father with weakness and insufficiency, as if it cannot extend so far as these things, but fails to fill that which is empty, and to dispel the shadow, and that when no one is offering any hindrance.[5]

5. Irenaeus, *Against Heresies*, II.viii.1-2, in *The Ante-Nicene Fathers*, ed. Alexander Roberts and James Donaldson (24 vols. Grand Rapids, 1953), 5, 368.

In spite of its association with Gnosticism and Irenaeus' attempt to reduce it to absurdity, the conception of the world as shadow continued to occupy a central position in Christian Neoplatonism, perhaps partly because of such statements in the Old Testament as David's "our days on the earth are as a shadow, and there is none abiding" (I Chron. 29:15). Be that as it may, the idea is found in St. Bonaventure, Nicholas of Cusa, Pico della Mirandola, and Ficino. Even in so stoutly orthodox a work as Thomas Wilson's *A Christian Dictionary* the word "shadow" is defined as "This whole world, and the things thereof. Psalm 39,6, and 73, 20. Rom. 12,2. 1 Cor. 7,31. 1 Joh. 2, 17. Being but as shadowes of heavenly and true happinesse."[6] Indeed, the notion was so commonplace in the Renaissance that Lambertus Danaeus, like Irenaeus, found it necessary to warn the orthodox. He had probably been reading Irenaeus as well as Nicholas of Cusa and the Italian Neoplatonists, for he attributes the idea that earthly realities are but shadows both to Plato and to Valentinian the Gnostic, against whom Irenaeus had directed much

6. Etienne Gilson, *The Philosophy of St. Bonaventure*, trans. Dom Illtyd Trethowan and F. J. Sheed (New York, 1938), pp. 210–12, 515, n.10; Nicolas Cusanus, *Of Learned Ignorance*, trans. Fr. Germain Heron (London, 1954), pp. 150, 158 (III.vii, III.x); Pico della Mirandola, *Heptaplus*, in *Edizione Nazionale Dei Classici Del Pensiero Italiano, 1* (Firenze, 1942), 184; Ficino, *Epistolae (Opera*, Basle, 1573), *1*, 659, quoted in Nesca Robb, *Neoplatonism of the Italian Renaissance* (London, 1935), p. 87; Thomas Wilson, *A Christian Dictionary* (London, 1612), s.v.

of his polemic. Like Irenaeus, Danaeus takes the metaphor literally:

> But what absurdities and inconveniences doe followe that opinion, marke. For they muste needes confesse that those thinges, these heavenly *ideae* and Patterns, whereof, by their Doctrine, these earthly things are shadowes, too bee bodies, which is an absurd thing. Neither can a bodily thing be an image of thinges that are meere spirituall. Moreover, all this whole most beutifull woorke of GOD, which is called the worlde, shalbee a fantasie, and a meere dreame, and not that thing which we suppose it to be: which is blasphemous.[7]

But the metaphor was too vigorous to be demolished like this, and the phrase continued to appear in writers of a Platonizing tendency, such as Valentine Weigelius, Sir Henry Vane, and Peter Sterry, not to mention Blake, Shelley, Coleridge, the Transcendentalists, and even Arthur Symons almost in our own day.[8]

7. *The Wonderfull Workmanship of the World* (London, 1578), p. 24a.

8. Weigelius, *ASTROLOGIE Theologized,* pp. 45–46; Jones, *Spiritual Reformers in the Sixteenth and Seventeenth Centuries,* p. 276 (on Vane); Vivian De Sola Pinto, *Peter Sterry: Platonist and Puritan* (Cambridge, Cambridge University Press, 1934), pp. 161–62; Blake, *Jerusalem,* 77; Shelley, *Prometheus Unbound,* II.iii.11–16; Coleridge, "The Destiny of Nations," vv. 12–25; *The Complete Essays and Other Writings of Ralph Waldo Emerson,* ed. Brooks Atkinson (New York, Modern Library, 1940, 1950), pp. 216, 284, and passim; Arthur Symons, *The Symbolist Movement in Literature* (New York, Dutton Everyman, 1958), pp. 95–96.

We have now to look at the word "shadow" in its Christian meaning of foreshadowing, adumbration, or type. This was, indeed, a much more common use of the word in the seventeenth century than the Neoplatonic meaning we have been discussing. It appears, for example, in the titles of Christopher Harvey's *Synagogue: or the Shadow of the Temple* (1640) and William Guild's popular handbook of types of Christ, *MOSES UNVAILED: OR THOSE FIGURES WHICH SERVED UNTO the patterne and shaddow of heavenly things* (1620). Examples abound in the religious literature of the time, and it would be pointless to multiply them. The interesting questions are how the word "shadow" came to have this specifically Christian meaning and what connection, if any, there is between this and the Neoplatonic conception.

The word *skia* occurs three times in the New Testament in the sense of type or foreshadowing:

> Let no man therefore judge you in meat, or in drink, or in respect of an holyday, or of the new moon, or of the sabbath days:
> Which are a shadow of things to come; but the body is of Christ. (Col. 2:16–17)

> Now of the things which we have spoken this is the sum: We have such an high priest, who is set on the right hand of the throne of the Majesty in the heavens;
> A minister of the sanctuary, and of the true tabernacle, which the Lord pitched, and not man.
> For every high priest is ordained to offer gifts and

95

sacrifices: wherefore it is of necessity that this man have somewhat also to offer.

For if he were on earth, he should not be a priest, seeing that there are priests that offer gifts according to the law:

Who serve unto the example and shadow of heavenly things, as Moses was admonished of God when he was about to make the tabernacle: for, See, saith he, that thou make all things according to the pattern shewed to thee in the mount. (Heb. 8:1–5)

For the law having a shadow of good things to come, and not the very image of the things, can never with those sacrifices which they offered year by year continually make the comers thereunto perfect. (Heb. 10:1)

These are not the only typological passages in the New Testament, of course, but they are the only ones in which the word *skia* is used. What metaphor did Paul in Colossians and the author of Hebrews have in mind? Sixteenth- and seventeenth-century commentators took "shadow" here to mean either "shadow cast by a body" or "silhouette or outline, as in painting." In both cases there is a simple analogy of proportion: as type is to antitype, so is the shadow to the body or substance, or the first draft of a picture to the finished painting. Calvin, with his usual clarity, distinguishes between the analogies in Colossians 2:17 and Hebrews 10:1.

For the law having the shadow, &c] He borrows this
similitude from the art of painting: for he takes this
word *shadow* in this place, otherwise than it is taken,
Col. 2.17, where S. *Paul* calles the old ceremonies,
shadows, because they had not the very substance of
the things in them, which they did represent. But the
Apostle saith here, they were like rude draughts,
which are but the shadows of the lively painting. For
painters are wont to drawe that which they purpose to
counterfeit or represent with a cole, before they set
on the lively colors with the pensill. The Apostle
then puts this difference betweene the law and the
Gospell: to wit, that that which at this day is drawne
and painted with fresh and lively colours, was onely
shadowed out under the law by a rude or grosse
draught.[9]

David Dickson and William Jones make use of both
analogies in commenting on Hebrews 10:1.

The revealing of Christ, and his Benefites, under the
Gospell, and under the Lawe, differ as farre in measure of light, as the shadowe of a thing, and the lyvelie
image thereof, drawne with all the lineamentes. For,
they sawe Christ, and Righteousnesse, and aeternall
Lyfe through him, as those which are in the house see

9. *A Commentarie on the Whole Epistle to the Hebrewes* (London,
1605), pp. 200–01. Professor Walter MacKellar has called my attention to
the gloss on "shadow" in Heb. 10:1 in the Geneva Bible: "which was as it
were the first draught and purtrait of the lively paterne to come."

the shadowe of a man comming, before hee enter within the doores: but, wee, with open face, beholde in
the Gospell, as in a Mirrour, Christ's Glorie shyning;
Christ, in the preaching of his word, crucified before
our Eyes, as it were, and bringing with him Lyfe, and
Immortalitie, to light.

So in the Law they had a sight of *Christ,* yet it was
darkly in a shadow. Wee have the very expresse forme
and image of *Christ,* with all his benefits: they had
Christ in an obscure picture drawne at the first in
darke lines: wee have him as in a lively picture graced
with most lightsome and excellent colours.[10]

Recent commentators, however, have seen in these passages in Hebrews the Platonic doctrine of the world as
image or copy. The author of Hebrews, says Alexander C.
Purdy in *The Interpreter's Bible,* "is controlled by a two-
story view of reality: on the ground floor the shadowy,
transient, fugitive events and institutions; in the upper
story the permanent, perfect realm of reality." And again,
"The idea of a realm of reality over against the shadowy
realm presented by our senses is clearly Platonic, but, of
course, this does not mean that our author had read Plato
or that he was a philosopher like Plato. It means that his
Christian convictions are presented in the atmosphere of

10. David Dickson, *A Short Explanation of Paul to the Hebrewes*
(Aberdeene, 1635), p. 197; William Jones, *A Commentary Upon the Epistles
of Saint Paul to Philemon and to the Hebrewes* (London, 1635), p. 383.

Platonic idealism."[11] If the author of Hebrews was the first to present his Christian convictions in the atmosphere of Platonic idealism, he was certainly not the last. In spite of the historic association between Christianity and the Attic Moses, however, there is a fundamental opposition between these two world-views that is already apparent in Hebrews. It is the opposition between the historical, eschatological spirit of Christianity implicit in the phrase "shadow of good things to come" and the nonhistorical, ontological spirit of Platonism. A typical Platonizing Jew like Philo saw in the Old Testament not the progressive revelation of God's purpose in the types and shadows of the Old Law, but rather allegories of subjective moral and religious experience or of Platonic archetypes. For the Gnostics Christ was not a Redeemer but an Illuminator, a Neoplatonic intermediary between the intelligible and the sensible realms rather than an actor in the divine drama of salvation.[12] The Epistle to the Hebrews, on the

11. *The Interpreter's Bible* (12 vols. New York, 1955), *11*, 583–84, 585. See also E. C. Rust, *The Christian Understanding of History* (London, 1947), pp. 174–78. Arndt & Gingrich's *A Greek-English Lexicon of the New Testament* (Chicago, 1952) defines *skia* as "2. shadow, foreshadowing (in contrast to reality)" and cites parallels from Philo Judaeus that are decidedly Platonic in implication. None of the modern commentaries or lexicons that I have consulted makes use of the analogy from painting. That the word was so used in ancient times is attested by Liddell and Scott: "III.1. shadow in painting 2. silhouette, profile."

12. I am indebted here to C. K. Barrett, "The Eschatology of the Epistle to the Hebrews," in *The Background of the New Testament and Its Eschatology*, ed. W. D. Davies and D. Daube (Cambridge, Cambridge

other hand, is profoundly eschatological. The author's gaze, as Father Prat has said, "is constantly turned towards the future, and the events of Jewish history are the book in which he reads the destiny of the heavenly Jerusalem, unchangeable and eternal." Or as a recent Protestant scholar has said, for the author of Hebrews "what lies between heaven and earth, God and man, is not the difference between the phenomena of sense-perception and pure being, but the difference between holiness and sin."[13]

The scholarly controversy over the philosophical orientation of Hebrews presents in its most striking form the radical divergence of meaning and implication inherent in the word "shadow." The Platonist who says that earth is the shadow of Heaven is saying (among other things) that history has no meaning. Things on earth have meanings, no doubt, but the meanings are static. It is not in their dynamic relationships with each other, as events in history, that earthly things have meaning; rather it is in their analogical relationships or their physical properties, and the world is a kind of symbolic pageant or emblem. On the

---

University Press, 1946). Robert M. Grant, on the other hand, thinks that the difference between Philo and the author of Hebrews lies not in method but in purpose. Philo wants to find God and the soul; the author of Hebrews wants to find Jesus. One finds philosophical allegory; the other predictive allegory *(The Letter and the Spirit* [New York, 1957], p. 55).

13. Fernand Prat, S.J., *The Theology of Saint Paul*, trans. from the 11th French ed. by John L. Stoddard (2 vols. Westminster, Md., 1926), *1,* 361; Barrett, p. 388.

other hand, the Christian who says that earth is the shadow (that is, foreshadowing) of Heaven is asserting the validity of history. The world is a stage on which the drama of salvation is enacted, and earthly things have meaning primarily in the context of history.[14] In Platonic and Neoplatonic thought man's nature is defined by the rational categories of Being and Becoming, the intelligible and the sensible; his immersion in the meaningless cycle of time is a misfortune, and the duty of man is to become a philosopher and thereby escape from the world. In Christian thought man is defined primarily by moral categories, and the Platonic distinction between the intelligible and the sensible is replaced by the Christian distinction between the Creator and His creation; man's immersion in time is the condition of his salvation, and the duty of man is to become a saint and thereby redeem the world.

In the Garden before the Fall Adam exists, as it were, outside of history, exempt from the limitations of time. There is, of course, movement in Adam's universe, as Joseph Summers has shown,[15] but it is Platonic cyclic movement, not Christian linear movement. It is the "Grateful vicissitude" of the "perpetual round" of light and darkness (VI.6–8). There is no real change in Paradise, only "interchange" (IX.115). Even Raphael's speculation (in one of his few references to the future) about the destiny of unfallen man is Neoplatonic:

14. See Emile Brehier, *The Philosophy of Plotinus*, trans. Joseph Thomas (Chicago, 1958), pp. 17–18.

15. *The Muse's Method* (Cambridge, Mass., 1962), Chap. 3.

> time may come when men
> With Angels may participate, and find
> No inconvenient Diet, nor too light Fare:
> And from these corporal nutriments perhaps
> Your bodies may at last turn all to spirit,
> Improv'd by tract of time, and wing'd ascend
> Ethereal, as wee, or may at choice
> Here or in Heav'nly Paradises dwell. (V.493–500)

This is the familiar Neoplatonic doctrine of the vertical ascent through the scale of being, not the horizontal journey through the "tract of time" that fallen mankind will have to make.

"All teems with symbol," said Plotinus,[16] and this apparently Neoplatonic garden is indeed a forest of symbols, paradoxically typological and prophetic, not Platonic; they speak of what lies ahead, not what lies above; they are a shadow of things to come. The rivers of Paradise, for example, do not stand for the four cardinal virtues, as they do in Henry More's allegorical interpretation,[17] which is in the Platonizing manner of Philo Judaeus, but in their movements they foreshadow the Fall and man's subsequent wanderings:

> Southward through *Eden* went a River large,
> Nor chang'd his course, but through the shaggy hill
> Pass'd underneath ingulft, for God had thrown
> That Mountain as his Garden mould high rais'd

16. *Enneads,* II.iii.7.
17. *Conjectura,* p. 38.

Upon the rapid current, which through veins
Of porous Earth with kindly thirst up-drawn,
Rose a fresh Fountain, and with many a rill
Water'd the Garden; thence united fell
Down the steep glade, and met the nether Flood,
Which from his darksome passage now appears,
And now divided into four main Streams,
Runs diverse, wand'ring many a famous Realm
And Country whereof here needs no account.

(IV.223–35)

The trees "weep"; the serpent, even before Satan enters
him, "of his fatal guile / Gave proof unheeded"; the "steep
wilderness" on the side of the mount of Paradise foreshadows the wilderness of this world to which Adam and
Eve must descend after their trespass; Eve's dream is prophetic, and Adam wakes from his to find "all real, as the
dream / Had lively shadow'd" (VIII.310–11). One of the
most interesting examples of typological symbolism in the
Garden is Eve's recital to Adam of how in her first moments of existence she gazed at her own image in the water.
She would have pined with vain desire until now, she
says, if a voice had not thus warned her:

What thou seest,
What there thou seest fair Creature is thyself,
With thee it came and goes: but follow me,
And I will bring thee where no shadow stays
Thy coming, and thy soft imbraces, hee
Whose image thou art   (IV.467–72)

She followed the voice, but she thought Adam less fair than the "smooth wat'ry image" and turned away from him. You called me back, she tells him, and

> thy gentle hand
> Seiz'd mine, I yielded, and from that time see
> How beauty is excell'd by manly grace
> And wisdom, which alone is truly fair.
>
> (IV.488–91)

When Adam explains to Eve that manly grace and wisdom are to physical beauty what physical reality is to its shadow, he is drawing the obvious lesson from Eve's experience. But there is another meaning that entirely escapes Adam. There is a foreshadowing as well as a shadow here, and it is a foreshadowing of Adam's own sin (not of Eve's, as is so often said). When he determines to throw in his lot with Eve, he is choosing the physical shadow over the moral substance. He has seen his image in her, just as Satan saw his image in Sin, and he turns from God to Eve, as Eve had turned from Adam to her own shadow in the water.

After the Fall a further typological significance of Paradise is revealed. "See Father," says Christ after Adam and Eve have repented,

> See Father, what first fruits on Earth are sprung
> From thy implanted Grace in Man, these Sighs
> And Prayers, which in this Golden Censer, mixt
> With Incense, I thy Priest before thee bring,
> Fruits of more pleasing savor from thy seed

Sown with contrition in his heart, than those
Which his own hand manuring all the Trees
Of Paradise could have produc't, ere fall'n
From innocence.   (XI.22–30)

This passage, which contains as high a concentration of
metaphors as any in the poem, and which uses language
drawn both from the Garden ("fruits," "implanted,"
"sown") and from Old Testament ceremonialism ("Censer," "incense," "Priest"), is a kind of paradigm of the
linguistic enactment of the ascent "From shadowy Types
to Truth," and it will be worthwhile to dwell on it for a
moment.

The references to priest and censer here and elsewhere
in *Paradise Lost* and the fact that Heaven is imaged as a
temple in which sanctuary lights burn before an altar and
the angelic host performs the functions of a monastic choir,
together with Milton's use of royalist imagery in referring to God and Christ, have seemed to some critics to
support the contention that the Catholic, royalist, symbolic
statements of *Paradise Lost* contradict the Protestant, re-
publican, "prose" statements.[18] Since the sensuous desert
of Puritanism had no symbols to offer Milton, it is said,
he returned to the fleshpots of Egypt, plundering the rich
treasure house of Catholic ritual and royalist ceremony. A
moment's reflection on the doctrine of typology, however,
will convince us that Milton is not cheating. The symbols

18. Malcolm M. Ross, *Milton's Royalism* (Ithaca, N.Y., 1943) and *Poetry
and Dogma* (New Brunswick, 1954), passim.

of royalty, of priesthood and sacrifice, of altars, incense, and sanctuary lights come not from Catholicism, Anglicanism, or the English monarchy, but from the religious ceremonies of the Old Testament, which were instituted by God. There is a sense, indeed, in which it can be said that Milton is not using the language of the Old Testament metaphorically. No doubt words such as "incense" and "censer" must be regarded as metaphors from any point of view, but if we call "priest" and "king" metaphors we are making the same mistake that Satan makes in *Paradise Regained* when he says that if Christ's kingdom is not to be physical it must be "allegoric." Milton is using these words in their primary, nonmetaphorical, "God-given" sense, as it were.[19] There is no earthly king because Christ is the only King; there is no earthly priest because Christ is the true Priest; there is no earthly sacrifice because Christ offered once and for all the supreme sacrifice. The flesh of the Old Testament has become the words of *Paradise Lost*.

In the language drawn from the Garden in the passage

19. Perhaps the statement in the text should be modified in the light of Aquinas' distinction between the perfections signified by the names of God and their mode of signification: "Therefore as to the names applied to God, there are two things to be considered—namely, the perfections which they signify, such as goodness, life, and the like, and their mode of signification. As regards what is signified by these names, they belong properly to God, and more properly than they belong to creatures, and are applied primarily to Him. But as regards their mode of signification, they do not properly and strictly apply to God, for their mode of signification applies to creatures" *(S.T.*, I, Q. 13, Art. 3).

under discussion there is no question of "sacred metaphor" or of a world in which physical areas have moral meaning or in which objects are "saturated with the 'meaning' that we usually apply to [them] from outside." The unfallen world of *Paradise Lost* is not a world in which the spatial and moral meanings of the word "high" are synonymous, nor is it a world that is "obedient still to the simple design of creation where, in Spenser's neo-Platonic phrase, 'all that fair is, is by nature good.' "[20] The language of Christ's address to the Father is possible because of a human act performed at the beginning of history. Only by the act of sin that destroyed the Garden could the Garden come to be seen as a type of the spiritual life. Adam could not know that his cultivation of the Garden was a shadow of things to come, and only the Word of God makes it possible for us to know it.

If the Garden foreshadowed the Fall of man, the Wilderness foreshadows his restoration in Christ, though it is now in the laws and ceremonies instituted by God rather than in the book of nature that man's future may be read by those who have eyes to see. The law was given to the Jews, Michael explains to Adam,

> With purpose to resign them in full time
> Up to a better Cov'nant, disciplin'd
> From shadowy Types to Truth, from Flesh to Spirit,
> From imposition of strict Laws, to free

20. MacCaffrey, Paradise Lost *as "Myth,"* pp. 68, 71.

Acceptance of large Grace, from servile fear
To filial, works of Law to works of Faith.

(XII.301–06)

With the coming of Christ all types are abolished; the shadow gives way to the substance, the rough draft to the lively image. "All corporeal resemblances of inward holiness and beauty are now past,"[21] said Milton in attacking the liturgy and hierarchy of the Anglican church. The only temple is the upright heart and pure, and the natural types of the Garden and the ceremonial types of the Wilderness are fulfilled spiritually in the minds and hearts of Christians. We are confronted here with a paradox. Insofar as the Old Testament contained the shadow of things to come and the New Testament the substance, the new dispensation has more validity, more meaning, than the old. From another point of view, however, human history before the coming of Christ has a meaning that history after His coming cannot possibly have; before Christ the world was charged with the grandeur of God's symbolic, typological drama; after Christ there is Michael's dreary vision of a world apparently emptied of significance and given over to Satan. What, we might ask, is the meaning of life on this earth now, in this last age of the world's history?

It is a difficult question to answer. Malcolm Ross for one thinks there is no meaning. Milton's God, he says

21. *Reason of Church Government*, II.ii, *SM*, p. 528.

bluntly, has abandoned history,[22] but Milton did not always think so, he points out. In the early days of his revolutionary enthusiasm Milton could look forward to the Second Coming of the "eternal and shortly expected King"[23] and could couch his expectation in the familiar terms of the Exodus typology:

> O perfect and accomplish thy glorious acts! for men may leave their works unfinished, but thou art a God, thy nature is perfection: shouldst thou bring us thus far onward from Egypt to destroy us in this wilderness, though we deserve, yet thy great name would suffer in the rejoicing of thine enemies, and the deluded hope of all thy servants. When thou hast settled peace in the church, and righteous judgment in the kingdom, then shall all thy saints address their voices of joy and triumph to thee, standing on the shore of that Red Sea into which our enemies had almost driven us.[24]

Young Milton's faith that God would not allow His name to suffer in the rejoicing of His enemies finds its parallel in Adam's confidence that God would not carry out His threat of death

> lest the Adversary
> Triumph and say; Fickle their State whom God

22. Ross, p. 106.
23. *Of Reformation, SM,* p. 469.
24. *Animadversions, SM,* p. 493. There is an interesting study of the Exodus typology in early Christian thought in Daniélou, *From Shadows to Reality.*

Most Favors, who can please him long? Mee first
He ruin'd, now Mankind; whom will he next?
Matter of scorn, not to be given the Foe.   (IX.947–51)

But God did sentence Adam to death, and He did allow
His English to return to the fleshpots of Egypt. With the
restoration of Charles II it would seem, as Ross wittily
remarks, that God had changed His mind.[25]

I do not think that this is the way Milton saw it, however.
The attitude with which the mature Milton confronted
the "contrived corridors and issues" of history, especially
the failure of the Commonwealth, is dramatically realized
in Raphael's account of the War in Heaven. The purpose
of Raphael's narrative is not merely to demonstrate to
Adam the consequences of disobedience; a recital of the
first two books of *Paradise Lost* would have been a much
more effective means to that end. Nor is its purpose to reveal that there is a Platonic idea of War in Heaven, of
which mere earthly wars are an imperfect embodiment.[26]
Milton, I venture to say, is not really interested in the particulars—if there were any particulars—of Satan's first
battle with God. What he is interested in, and what he
wants his readers to be interested in, is Raphael's *account*
of that war, which is a different matter. Raphael's account
is not a moral allegory, nor is it primarily a metaphorical
description of what happened a long time ago in Heav-

25. Ross, *Poetry and Dogma,* p. 106.
26. James Holly Hanford, "Milton and the Art of War," *SP, 18* (1921),
232–66.

en.[27] It is a shadow of things to come, and more particularly it is a shadow of this last age of the world and of the Second Coming of Christ.[28]

The world is not only a waste wilderness in which the spiritual Eden is re-created in the minds of the regenerate, but it is also a battlefield, the scene of "th' invisible exploits / Of warring Spirits" (V.565–66). Recent critics have elucidated some of the moral meanings that the War in Heaven can have—obedience to the will of God, discipline, freedom of choice. In my opinion, however, the principal lesson that Raphael's narrative inculcates is the lesson of patience, the virtue with which the Christian confronts the perplexities of history. It is one of the most difficult virtues to practice, as difficult for Milton as it was for some of the good angels. If the youthful Milton had taken part in the War in Heaven, we can imagine him fervently assenting with Abdiel:

O Heav'n! that such resemblance of the Highest
Should yet remain, where faith and realty

27. It is, of course, simply a fiction that Raphael is "measuring things in Heav'n by things on Earth" (VI.893), and it is absurd to claim that Milton here actually employs the method of accommodation. Because of the impossibility of looking behind the narrative to the actual conflict in Heaven (whatever its nature, about which Milton had no more special knowledge than anyone else) I have regarded its significance as primarily, though not exclusively, typological, that is, oriented toward the future.

28. For evidence that Ezekiel's vision, which Milton incorporates in his description of Christ's rout of the rebel angels, was regarded as a foreshadowing of Christ's re-creation of the universe on the Last Day, see J. H. Adamson, "The War in Heaven: Milton's Version of the *Merkabah*," *JEGP*, 57 (1958), 690–703.

Remain not; wherefore should not strength and might
There fail where Virtue fails, or weakest prove
Where boldest; though to sight unconquerable?
His puissance, trusting in th' Almighty's aid,
I mean to try, whose Reason I have tri'd
Unsound and false; nor is it aught but just,
That he who in debate of Truth hath won,
Should win in Arms, in both disputes alike
Victor; though brutish that contest and foul,
When Reason hath to deal with force, yet so
Most reason is that Reason overcome.   (VI.114–26)

If this were only true, history would offer no perplexities, and God's purposes could be read in the rise and fall of empires. And when Abdiel's "noble stroke" sent Satan recoiling, one can imagine the youthful Milton in-the very forefront of the angelic host, filled with "Presage of Victory and fierce desire / Of Battle" (VI.201–02), just as he had been in the forefront of those who saw in the Puritan Revolution a presage of the Millennium. But Abdiel was wrong: his reason did not overcome Satan's might, and the first blow struck against evil did not end the war. From the reader's point of view the outcome of the struggle is never in doubt because he is privileged to see it under the aspect of eternity. This vision is not granted to the angelic participants, however, and after their "forc't rout" by Satan's cannon, the good angels "stood / A while in trouble" (VI.633–34). For them the outcome hangs in the balance for two long days (and a day is to God as a thousand years), and the war would have gone on forever had not God intervened in His good time. The War in Heaven lasts until Christ appears and drives the rebel angels into Hell, and the world goes on "To good malignant, to bad men benign," until Christ comes at last "to dissolve / *Satan* with his perverted World" (XII.538, 546–47), because patience is the exercise of saints. Patience is not a kind of spiritual setting-up exercise arbitrarily imposed on us by God. It is necessary because we are creatures living in a world we did not create and immersed in a time process that is the fulfillment of a purpose not our own. We must act, assuredly. We must put on the whole armor of God and wrestle against principalities and the rulers of darkness, as the good angels did, but we must abide the time. Whatever else the restoration of Charles II meant to Milton, it did not mean that God had changed His mind and abandoned history. The typological meaning of Paradise was not revealed until it had been destroyed, nor the meaning of the Old Testament dispensation until it had been abrogated. So too the meaning of this last age will be fully revealed when Christ's mystical body has grown to its full stature and the righteous have entered into the state of "perfect glorification."[29] Meanwhile we live in a time that is intersected by eternity, and our actions on earth are shadows of Heaven—or of Hell.

The Scale of Nature

Well hast thou taught the way that might direct
Our knowledge, and the scale of Nature set

29. *Christian Doctrine*, I.xxxiii, *SM*, pp. 1046–48.

From centre to circumference, whereon
In contemplation of created things
By steps we may ascend to God.   (V.508–12)

We must now examine in more detail the Neoplatonic idea of the ascent of the soul alluded to briefly in the discussion of the analogy of the Line and the Cave. In this passage from the *Republic,* as well as in the *Symposium* and other dialogues, Plato speaks of the intellectual progress of the philosopher as an ascent of the soul from the sensible realm to the intelligible, from the realm of shadows to that of reality, from the world of Becoming to the world of Being. Whether there are elements of genuine religious mysticism in these passages is debated by students of Plato; in any case, his teachings were interpreted in a religious sense by Plotinus and the Neoplatonists, who thus became the principal intermediaries between Plato and the Christian mystics.

Plotinus' universe is a graded hierarchy of being produced by necessary emanations from the One, a process that Plotinus sometimes images as the propagation of light that gets dimmer and dimmer as it gets farther away from its source. The first emanation is Intelligence (Nous), which is intuition having a twofold object—the One and Itself. In it exist the Ideas, and Plotinus identifies it with the Demiurge of the *Timaeus.* From Nous emanates Soul, which corresponds to the World-Soul of Plato. This is the link between the intelligible and sensible worlds, except that Plotinus, in an apparent effort to keep the intelligible as far from contamination by the material as possible, posits two souls: one closer to Nous and having no contact with the sensible world, and a second called *physis* or Nature, which is the real World-Soul. Individual human souls "descend" from the World-Soul to the material world.

Plotinus is hard put to explain the descent of the individual soul. In one breath he says that the individual souls in the World-Soul want to be independent, to assert their own individuality. In the next breath he says it is an eternal law of nature that souls descend into bodies for the good of the whole universe. Even so, the soul commits a wrong in thus descending, and its punishment is the descent itself. Once in the body, estranged from the whole, the soul "becomes a thing fragmented, isolated, and weak." "A thing fallen, chained, at first barred off from intelligence and living only by sensation, the soul is, as they say, in tomb or cavern pent. Yet its higher part remains. Let the soul, taking its lead from memory, merely 'think on essential being' and its shackles are loosed and it soars."[30]

Thus the soul begins its ascent to the One, the "flight of the alone to the Alone." As in Plato the ascent (which of course is a metaphor for what is better described as a turning inward of the soul to its inmost being) begins under the impulse of Eros with a process of purification, after which the soul rises above sense perception and occupies itself with philosophy and science. In the next stage the

30. *Enneads*, IV.viii.4–5.

soul rises above discursive thought and reaches the utter-
most limit of the Intelligible.[31] The final state, attained
only briefly in this life, is a mystical union with the One in
a kind of ecstasy or inebriation of the intellect.

If Plotinus turned what was essentially an intellectual
quest in Plato into a religious quest, Augustine refashions
Plotinus' quest into a Christian one, while retaining his
technique and the Platonic essentials.[32] Augustine of
course rejects Plotinian emanationism for the Christian
doctrine of *creatio ex nihilo,* and for Plotinus' rational
hierarchy of being he substitutes the hierarchy of matter-
spirit-God. The "ascent" of the soul, however, proceeds by
essentially the same steps. Characteristically, though not
necessarily, it begins with a recognition of the beauty and
order of the material universe, where certain traces or
footprints of God may be found, but it rapidly proceeds
inward to the mind, where the image of God may be discerned, especially in the trinity of memory-understanding-
will. By reflecting on the fact that the human mind makes
judgments that are immutably true, though it is itself not
immutable, Augustine proceeds to the knowledge that
there exists an immutable and eternal source of truth, who
is God.

Setting aside for the moment medieval variations on this
theme, let us glance at the speculations of the Florentine

31. Ibid., I.iii.1.
32. Etienne Gilson, *The Christian Philosophy of St. Augustine,* trans.
L. E. M. Lynch (New York, 1960), p. 256, n.36.

Neoplatonists, who speak of the soul's ascent in different terms at different times: from the objective form through the innate formula to the Idea and from there to the divine essence; from lowest causes through intermediary causes to God as highest cause; from lowest species to highest genera. Underlying these formulas are the Platonic distinction between the sensible world and the intelligible and the Platonic emphasis on detachment from matter. "Under God's guidance," says Ficino, "we shall arrive at the highest degree of nature if we separate the affection of our Soul as much as possible from matter, which is the lowest degree of nature, in order that we may approach God as much as we withdraw from matter." And again, "Through a natural eagerness for truth the mind separates itself continually from the body, and the forms from matter, and thus it desires and tries to live separately, though the body and the senses drive it daily to the contrary."[33]

Sometimes the ascent of the soul is presented as a literal journey upward through the hierarchy of being. In Pico's *Oration on the Dignity of Man,* for example, we read that

> the best of artisans ordained that that creature to whom He had been able to give nothing proper to himself should have joint possession of whatever had been peculiar to each of the different kinds of being.

33. *Opera omnia* (Basle, 1561), pp. 424, 186, quoted in Paul O. Kristeller, *The Philosophy of Marsilio Ficino* (New York, 1943), pp. 214, 215–16. Cf. Erasmus: "Let us not creep like vile insects upon earth; but raising ourselves often upon those wings which grow again in our minds, pushed out,

117

He therefore took man as a creature of indeterminate nature and, assigning him a place in the middle of the world, addressed him thus: 'Neither a fixed abode nor a form that is thine alone nor any function peculiar to thyself have we given thee, Adam, to the end that according to thy longing and according to thy judgment thou mayest have and possess what abode, what form, and what functions thou thyself shalt desire. The nature of all other beings is limited and constrained within the bounds of laws prescribed by Us. Thou, constrained by no limits, in accordance with thine own free will, in whose hand We have placed thee, shalt ordain for thyself the limits of thy nature. We have set thee at the world's center that thou mayest from thence more easily observe whatever is in the world. We have made thee neither of heaven nor of earth, neither mortal nor immortal, so that with freedom of choice and with honor, as though the maker and molder of thyself, thou mayest fashion thyself in whatever shape thou shalt prefer. Thou shalt have the power to degenerate into the lower forms of life, which are brutish. Thou shalt have the power, out of the

---

as *Plato* observes, by the genial warmth of Love, soar from Body to Spirit, from the visible World to the invisible, from the Letter to the Sense and Meaning, from sensible Objects to intelligible, from compounded to pure and simple: mounting thus step by step, as it were by *Jacob's* Ladder, from earth to heaven" (*The Christian's Manual. Being a Translation from the* Enchiridion Militis Christiani *of Erasmus* [London, 1752], p. 155).

soul's judgment, to be reborn into the higher forms, which are divine.'[34]

In his set piece on the scale of nature Raphael seems to echo this Neoplatonic doctrine:

> O *Adam,* one Almighty is, from whom
> All things proceed, and up to him return,
> If not deprav'd from good, created all
> Such to perfection, one first matter all,
> Indu'd with various forms, various degrees
> Of substance, and in things that live, of life;
> But more refin'd, more spiritous, and pure,
> As nearer to him plac't or nearer tending
> Each in thir several active Spheres assign'd,
> Till body up to spirit work, in bounds
> Proportion'd to each kind.
>
>   . . .
>
>   time may come when men
> With Angels may participate, and find
> No inconvenient Diet, nor too light Fare:

34. Trans. Elizabeth Forbes, in *The Renaissance Philosophy of Man,* ed. Ernst Cassirer and others (Chicago, University of Chicago Press, 1948), pp. 224–25. Cf. Oswald Crollius, *Philosophy Reformed & Improved* (London, 1657), p. 53: "Man who is a true *Proteus* of a fickle & wavering disposition received a flexible mind from Nature, that being set in the midst of the Paradice of this world, by the assistance of Divine Grace raising himselfe upward he might be regenerated into a quiet Angell or, the Forger of his fortune winding and creeping downward degenerate into a restlesse Bruite."

And from these corporal nutriments perhaps
Your bodies may at last turn all to spirit,
Improv'd by tract of time, and wing'd ascend
Ethereal, as wee, or may at choice
Here or in Heav'nly Paradises dwell;
If ye be found obedient, and retain
Unalterably firm his love entire
Whose progeny you are.   (V.469–79, 493–503)

The passage is heavily charged with ambivalence. The Neoplatonic doctrine of descent and return is clearly implied in the second line, but in the very next line "proceed," which suggests emanationism, is qualified by "created," and the idea of the return to God is qualified by "If not deprav'd from good." Some words suggest that the scale of nature is dynamic—"tending," "Till body up to spirit work," "Springs," "aspire," and "ascend"—but at the same time, it appears to be static: "plac't," "assign'd," "bounds." Finally, the whole conception of Adam's ascent to the condition of angels is shown to be irrelevant to man in his fallen state with the qualification "If ye be found obedient." Adam is not found obedient, and he does not ascend to God by steps "In contemplation of created things." Instead he falls, and when he is raised it is to a higher condition than the hypothetical one envisaged by Raphael. Speaking to the Son in Book III God says,

Thou therefore whom thou only canst redeem,
Thir Nature also to thy Nature join;

And be thyself Man among Men on Earth,
Made flesh, when time shall be, of Virgin seed,
By wondrous birth: Be thou in *Adam's* room
The Head of all mankind, though *Adam's* Son.
As in him perish all men, so in thee
As from a second root shall be restor'd,
As many as are restor'd, without thee none.
His crime makes guilty all his Sons, thy merit
Imputed shall absolve them who renounce
Thir own both righteous and unrighteous deeds,
And live in thee transplanted, and from thee
Receive new life.

    . . .

Nor shalt thou by descending to assume
Man's Nature, lessen or degrade thine own.

    . . .

         because in thee
Love hath abounded more than Glory abounds,
Therefore thy Humiliation shall exalt
With thee thy Manhood also to this Throne;
Here shalt thou sit incarnate, here shalt Reign
Both God and Man, Son both of God and Man,
Anointed universal King;

        (III.281–94, 303–04, 311–17)

In this definitive vision of the Incarnation Christ is not
merely the moral exemplar so many critics have seen in
Paradise Regained. He is the Head of mankind in Adam's
room; He is the second root; He is the new Garden in

121

which man will live transplanted; His descent into the flesh is the true pattern of the humiliation that exalts. Milton's metaphorical transformation of the Garden and his brilliant manipulations of the patterns of rising-to-fall and falling-to-rise in this passage and elsewhere in *Paradise Lost*[35] are possible not because moral value inheres in places or because God has miraculously reversed "the ordinary implications of his universal structure so that a descent becomes really the first step in an ascent";[36] they are possible because Christ is the symbolizing center of the poem. Neither places nor things have any inherent moral or spiritual meaning or value in *Paradise Lost,* or if they do, their meaning is ambiguous. Even the sacrosanct symbol of light is liable to certain ambiguous qualifications.[37] Its use was sanctioned for Milton by its definitive association with Christ in the Bible; on the other hand, its association with pagan sun-worship and its metaphoric use as an image of emanation by Plotinus imposed on Milton a delicate problem of symbolic manipulation. As a physical substance it is always good, like everything else created by God, but Raphael warns Adam that "Great / Or Bright infers not Excellence." The earth, which does not glister, "may of solid good contain / More plenty than the Sun that barren shines" (VIII.91–94). Although light is almost

35. This topic is suggestively discussed by Jackson I. Cope, *The Metaphoric Structure of* Paradise Lost (Baltimore, 1962), pp. 77–148.
36. MacCaffrey, Paradise Lost *as "Myth,"* p. 63.
37. Summers, *The Muse's Method,* p. 28.

always related to the "upper" regions of Milton's universe, it is significant that

> There is a Cave
> Within the Mount of God, fast by his Throne,
> Where light and darkness in perpetual round
> Lodge and dislodge by turns,

though, indeed, "darkness there might well / Seem twilight here" (VI.4–12). Raphael hedges because darkness, defined as the complete absence of light, is the one totally unambiguous symbol in *Paradise Lost*—unambiguous because it is, literally, nothing.

As for the symbolic meanings that cluster around words such as "high" and "low," it is true that movement toward God is usually "upward" movement and that the rebel angels are hurled "down / To bottomless perdition" (I.46–47). It is also true, however, that it is the fallen angels who subscribe to the view that "the place inhabited by a creature gives the key to its moral status, because moral values inhere in places."[38] Moloch argues that the "proper" motion of spirits is upward, and the devils who "reason'd high / Of Providence, Foreknowledge, Will, and Fate" "sat on a Hill retir'd, / In thoughts more elevate" (II.557–59). Satan sits "high on a Throne of Royal State" (II.1), and in *Paradise Regained*, when he places Christ on the pinnacle of the temple, he says, "I to thy Father's house

38. MacCaffrey, p. 69.

/ Have brought thee, and highest plac't, highest is best"
(PR, IV.552–53). Michael, on the other hand, tells Adam
that "God attributes to place / No sanctity" (XI.836–37).
In *Paradise Lost* meaning and value are extrinsic,

> So little knows
> Any, but God alone, to value right
> The good before him, but perverts best things
> To worst abuse, or to thir meanest use.   (IV.201–04)

Height may recall "high thoughts" (IV.95) in the sense of
proud thoughts, as it does with Satan, and it may be death-
dealing, as it is when Beelzebub says it is no wonder they
are astounded and amazed, "fall'n such a pernicious
highth" (I.282). In Neoplatonism descent is always nega-
tive, ascent always positive. In Christianity it all depends
on attitudes and contexts. Christ's descent into matter is
voluntary and redemptive, and his ascent is not an escape
from the flesh but a glorification of it. It is Satan who enacts
the Neoplatonic metaphor:

> O foul descent! that I who erst contended
> With Gods to sit the highest, am now constrain'd
> Into a Beast, and mixt with bestial slime,
> This essence to incarnate and imbrute,
> That to the highth of Deity aspir'd.   (IX.163–67)

The Book of Knowledge Fair

In the quotation from Adam which heads the preceding
section the ascent to God is associated with the "contem-

plation of created things." This theme adds a distinctly Hebraic and Christian note to the Neoplatonic ascent of the soul, but its Christian implications (which Adam, of course, is unaware of) have not always been noticed. For medieval Neoplatonists like the Victorines and St. Bonaventure meditation on the creatures as the first step in the ascent to God is not merely Neoplatonism with the doctrine of the Trinity added. What is distinctively Christian in their thought is their insistence that Christ is the symbolic center of the universe; He is the Incarnate Word revealed in the Bible and in the sacraments of the church. However frequently Neoplatonic metaphors such as "shadow" appear in medieval contemplations of nature, there is another metaphor that is even more pervasive and that bears witness to its Christian origin: the metaphor of the "book of nature."[39] Following are some characteristic examples of this metaphor from the twelfth to the seventeenth centuries.

> Omnis mundi creatura
> quasi liber et pictura
> nobis est in speculum,
> nostrae vitae, nostrae sortis,
> nostri status, nostrae mortis,
> fidele signaculum.

39. Harold Fisch would have it that "book of nature" is a "typical *logos* formula going back to Plato; the *cosmos* is visualized as a written, rationally comprehensible document." (No reference to Plato is supplied.) He goes on to say that in the seventeenth century the formula gets involved

Thus also in God the intrinsic word was the hidden and invisible word of His heart, and wisdom was this word; it was invisible, until it became manifest through the extrinsic word made visible, which was His work . . . . Wisdom was a book written within; the work of wisdom a book written without.

The first principle made the sensible world to make Himself known so that, as it were, by a vestige and a mirror man should be led back to loving God the artificer and to praising Him. In accord with this idea there is a double book, one written within which is the eternal art and wisdom of God, and the other written without, namely, the sensible world.

Il mondo è il libro dove il Senno Eterno
scrisse i propri concetti, e vivo tempio
dove, pingendo i gesti e 'l proprio esempio,
di statue vive ornò l'imo e 'l superno.

The World's a Book in *Folio,* printed all
With God's great Works in letters Capitall:
Each Creature is a Page; and each Effect
A fair Character, void of all defect.

----

with Hebraic motifs, so that the book of nature is often thought of as a Hebrew book and as such interchangeable with the Bible itself *(Jerusalem and Albion* [New York, 1964], p. 216, n.1). This puts the matter the wrong way. A written, rationally comprehensible document is precisely what the book of nature was not in medieval thought; it only becomes so in the scientific thought of the sixteenth and seventeenth centuries.

Philosophy is written in that great book which ever lies before our eyes—I mean the universe—but we cannot understand it if we do not first learn the language and grasp the symbols, in which it is written. This book is written in the mathematical language, and the symbols are triangles, circles, and other geometrical figures, without whose help it is impossible to comprehend a single word of it; without which one wanders in vain through a dark labyrinth.

There is no page in the book of nature unwritten on.

Thus there are two bookes from whence I collect my Divinity; besides that written one of God, another of his servant Nature, that universall and publik Manuscript, that lies expans'd unto the eyes of all.

Thrice happy he who, not mistook,
Hath read in *Natures mystick Book*.[40]

40. Alain de Lille, quoted in De Bruyne, *Études*, 2, 338; Hugh of St. Victor, *On the Sacraments of the Christian Faith*, trans. Roy J. Deferrari (Cambridge, Mass., 1951), I.iii.xx and I.vi.v; St. Bonaventure, *Breviloquium*, trans. E. E. Nemmers (St. Louis, 1947), II.xi.2; Thomas Campanella, quoted in Eugenio Garin, "Alcune Osservazioni sul *Libro* Come Simbolo," in *Umanesimo e Simbolismo* (Padova, 1958), p. 92; *Du Bartas His Divine Weekes and Workes*, in *The Complete Works of Joshuah Sylvester*, ed. A. B. Grosart, Chertsey Worthies' Library (2 vols. Edinburgh, 1880), *1*, 20; Galileo, quoted in E. A. Burtt, *The Metaphysical Foundations of Modern Science* (New York, Anchor Books, n.d.), p. 75; Thomas Adams, *Works*, Nichol's Standard Divines (Edinburgh, 1862), p. 175; Sir Thomas Browne, *Religio Medici*, ed. Jean-Jacques Denonain (Cambridge, Cambridge University Press, 1953), p. 24 (I.16); and Andrew Marvell, "Upon Appleton House," st. 73.

Like most metaphors with a long history, "book of nature" encompasses a bewildering variety of meanings. Bacon, who is fond of pouring new wine into old bottles, means something quite different from Bonaventure's understanding of what God has written in His external book, and Browne's imaginative apprehension of metaphoric and symbolic correspondences has little in common with the wooden analogies of Bellarmine. When Thomas Adams reads the book of nature, he uses as a gloss the imagery of the Bible, and the light of the sun puts him in mind of the light of glory; for Nicholas of Cusa, on the other hand, the visible world is symbolic of the invisible principally in its mathematical aspect, and his favorite symbols are not lambs and pelicans or rocks and rivers, but unity and multiplicity, the line and the circle.[41] I will try to impose some kind of order, however artificial and oversimplified, on this material by suggesting that most of the meanings attached to "book of nature" in the Middle Ages and Renaissance can be assigned to one or more of the following headings:

> Metaphoric, poetic, concrete
>> Hermeticism, doctrine of signatures
>> Bestiaries, lapidaries
>> Nature as a repository of symbols whose meaning is revealed only in the Bible
>> Nature as a metaphysical poem, composed of witty conceits

41. *Of Learned Ignorance,* esp. I.xi.

Literal, scientific, abstract

> Nature as an effect of God's power, wisdom, and goodness
>
> Nature as an example of God's attributes of order, harmony, and so on
>
> Nature as a book of mathematical symbols

This classification is not a logical one, since some of the categories overlap, and it is difficult to find a writer or even a work that falls under only one heading. The kind of imagination that finds expression in bestiaries and lapidaries is at its height in the early Middle Ages, but it continues to exert its influence on Franciscans like St. Bonaventure,[42] and its persistence if not its vitality is attested by its presence in the *Divine Weeks* of Du Bartas. The more philosophical conception of the creatures as a book that leads men to a contemplation of the ineffable mysteries of God (the reflection of the Trinity in the threefold powers of the soul, for example) gradually gives way in the sixteenth and seventeenth centuries to the scientific conception of nature as a book of mathematical signs whose contemplation leads not to ineffable mystery but to the rational and the explicable,[43] but even such scientists as Galileo and William Harvey, as Miss Nicholson has shown, were influenced by medieval ideas of symbolic correspondence.[44] In spite of these overlappings and ambi-

42. Etienne Gilson, *The Spirit of Medieval Philosophy,* trans. A. H. C. Downes (New York, 1936), pp. 100–01.

43. Garin, "Alcune Osservazioni," p. 96.

44. Nicholson, *The Breaking of the Circle,* Chap. 4.

guities, however, there is a clear movement from the symbolic and religious emphasis of the Middle Ages to the more literal and scientific emphasis of the seventeenth century.

Most Christians, from St. Augustine to Milton, believe that the natural man cannot understand the book of nature. Although there is a tradition of theocentric (as opposed to Christocentric) contemplation which "consists in contemplation of God as He is reflected in created things, and a gradual ascent from them to God,"[45] in actual practice most of these treatises presuppose an audience of Christians who already believe in God and are familiar with the Bible. Even Bellarmine's *De ascensione mentis,* which is as purely theocentric as possible, consists largely of analogies between sensible things and the attributes of God, Whose existence is taken for granted. Bellarmine divides his treatise into fifteen steps, "in resemblance of the fifteene steps by the which they went up into the Temple of Salomon, and of the fifteene Psalmes which are called Gradualles."[46] He begins with the consideration of man and then moves to the greater world, the earth, water, air, fire, the heavenly bodies, the reasonable soul (in which he finds an "obscure image" of the Trinity), and the angels. The last six steps consider God's essence, power, wisdom,

45. Joseph Collins, *Christian Mysticism in the Elizabethan Age* (Baltimore, 1940), p. 45.

46. *A Most Learned and Pious Treatise, Full of Divine and Humane Philosophy, Framing a Ladder, Wherby Our Mindes May Ascend to God, by the Stepps of His Creatures* . . . , trans. T. B. Gent (Douai, 1616), A12r.

practical wisdom, mercy, and justice "by the similitude of a corporall quantitie," that is, by likening various attributes of God to breadth (immensity), length (eternity), height (omnipotency), and depth (incomprehensibility). It is clear that the metaphor of ascent, which in some varieties of Neoplatonism refers to an actual change in the soul's status or mode of being, applies to Bellarmine's arrangement of his materials. At each of the fifteen steps the mind "ascends" to God simply by thinking of Him in either a real or a metaphoric relation to some created thing.

Other Christian writers who discuss the book of nature are more explicit than Bellarmine about the inability of the natural man to understand it. Because the philosophers of the Gentiles investigated the works of creation with superstitious curiosity, says Hugh of St. Victor, their speculations were vain. Christian philosophers, on the other hand, ponder the works of salvation and drive away all vanity.[47] In the seventh book of the *Didascalicon,* which De Bruyne calls the first aesthetic treatise of the Middle Ages, Hugh says that

> this whole visible world is as a book written by the finger of God, that is, created by divine power; and individual creatures are as figures therein not devised by human will but instituted by divine authority to show forth the wisdom of the invisible things of God. But just as some illiterate man who sees an open

47. *De arca Noe morali,* IV.vi, quoted in *The Didascalicon of Hugh of St. Victor,* trans. Jerome Taylor (New York, 1961), p. 173, n.168.

131

book looks at the figures but does not recognize the letters: just so the foolish natural man who does not perceive the things of God sees outwardly in these visible creatures the appearances but does not inwardly understand the reason. But he who is spiritual and can judge all things, while he considers outwardly the beauty of the work inwardly conceives how marvelous is the wisdom of the Creator.[48]

In his treatise *On the Sacraments* Hugh draws an analogy between the spoken word, which manifests a man's wisdom, and the visible creation, which manifests the wisdom of God. Because of the Fall man is unable to see the spiritual significance of this outer book, and therefore God made a second work, Jesus Christ, "that wisdom might be seen more manifestly and be recognized more perfectly, that the eye of man might be illumined to the second writing, since it had been darkened to the first."[49]

This same emphasis on Christ as the symbolic center of the universe and on the Word of God by which Christ is revealed is found in the classic *Itinerarium* of St. Bonaventure.[50] Here there are six stages of ascension to God, symbolized by the six days of creation, the six steps to the

48. *Patrologia Latina*, 176.814, quoted by Charles Singleton, *Dante Studies I* (Cambridge, Mass., 1954), p. 25. See De Bruyne, *Études*, 2, 238ff.
49. *On the Sacraments*, I.vi.v.
50. *The Mind's Road to God*, trans. George Boas (New York, Liberal Arts Press, 1953). For a discussion of the book of nature in St. Bonaventure see George H. Tavard, *Transiency and Permanence* (St. Bonaventure, N.Y., 1954), Chap. 3.

throne of Solomon, and the six wings of the seraphim; these six stages correspond to six aspects of the soul's powers—sense, imagination, reason, intellect, intelligence, and synteresis (the apex of the mind). Sense and imagination are those powers of the soul that have reference to man's physical body; reason and intellect refer to the mind as it looks inward upon itself; and intelligence and synteresis refer to the mind as it looks above itself. In each of these stages of the soul's journey to God Bonaventure sees "shadows" and "vestiges" of the Trinity. In the first stage, for example, the power, wisdom, and benevolence of God shine forth in created things "as the carnal sense reports trebly to the inner sense." In the second stage Bonaventure perceives an analogy between the way sensible things enter the mind of man not in their substances but only in their images or similitudes and "the eternal generation of the Word, the Image, and the Son, eternally emanating from God the Father." In the third stage the mind is led to the Trinity by considering its threefold powers of memory, intellect, and will.

> From memory arises intelligence as its offspring, for then do we know when a likeness which is in the memory leaps into the eye of the intellect, which is nothing other than a word. From memory and intelligence is breathed forth love, which is the tie between the two.[51]

51. *The Mind's Road to God*, III.5.

Bonaventure ends his discussion of the traces of God in the sensible world by saying that there are four ways in which an effect is the sign of its cause and the exemplification of the exemplar: partly from its proper representation, partly from prophetic prefiguration, partly from angelic operation, and partly from further ordination:

> For every creature is by nature a sort of picture and likeness of that eternal wisdom, but especially that which in the book of Scripture is elevated by the spirit of prophecy to the prefiguration of spiritual things. But more does the eternal wisdom appear in those creatures in whose likeness God wished to appear in angelic ministry. And most specially does it appear in those which He wished to institute for the purpose of signifying which are not only signs according to their common name but also Sacraments.[52]

Bonaventure was keenly alive to sensuous beauty, but it is clear that immediate aesthetic apprehension is but the first imperfect and fleeting stage of the mind's ascent to God, to be quickly left behind in a consideration of the mind's inward powers. It is also clear that nature provides concrete symbols of the spiritual mainly through the medium of the Bible and the sacraments of the church, or, to use terms that will be prominent in the next chapter, the visual image is subordinated to the word.

The Christocentric nature of Bonaventure's theory of symbolic contemplation becomes even clearer in the fourth

52. Ibid., II.12.

stage, where fallen man, however much he may be illuminated by the light of nature and of acquired science, "cannot enter into himself that he may delight in the Lord in himself, unless Christ be his mediator."[53] It is only when man believes in, hopes in, and loves Jesus Christ that he recovers spiritual hearing and vision and his inner senses are renewed. In this stage of the ascent we ought especially to consider Holy Scripture as it reveals Christ, the uncreated Word, Who is both the beginning from which all things proceed and the end toward which all things tend. For Bonaventure, as for most medieval theologians, it is Christ Who gives symbolic meaning to created things, and it is principally in the Bible and in the sacraments that these meanings are revealed. Bonaventure even went so far as to regard red as the most beautiful of colors because it signified the Passion, and he thought that scars made the body more beautiful.[54]

The biblical and Christocentric nature of most orthodox meditations on the creatures is also apparent in the sixteenth and seventeenth centuries. Even Erasmus, whose thought is heavily tinged with a Neoplatonic contempt of the visible world, urges the Christian reader to

> compare the objects that strike upon his Senses, either
> to the angelical world; or, which is better, to that part
> of him that bears the nearest resemblance thereto;

53. Ibid., IV.2.

54. Sister Emma Jane Marie Spargo, *The Category of the Aesthetic in the Philosophy of Saint Bonaventure* (St. Bonaventure, N.Y., 1953), pp. 61, 68.

drawing lessons of morality from every thing that presents itself to his inspection . . . . When your eyes are delighted with the glorious prospect of the Sun rising in a morning, and with his beams gladning the whole earth; then think of the happiness of the heavenly Host, whose bright eternal Sun rises continually, but never sets. . . . Recollect parallel passages of Scripture, in which *Light* is almost every where a type of the Grace of God.[55]

Calvin, like Hugh of St. Victor, can see in "the creatures, as in so many mirrors, the infinite riches of [God's] wisdom, justice, goodness, and power," but he too warns that men taught only by nature have "no certain, sound, or distinct knowledge" of God. Even Plato, "the most religious and judicious" of the philosophers, "loses himself in his round globe." Therefore we need another and better assistance, which is Scripture.[56] In the devotional writings and sermons of the seventeenth century contemplation of the creatures is found to be almost always associated with the Word. William Perkins says that an example of the spiritual use of indifferent things guaranteed to us by Christian liberty is

when we take occasion by the creatures to meditate and speake of heavenly things: as, upon the sight of the

55. *The Christian's Manual* (London, 1752), pp. 107–09.
56. *Institutes of the Christian Religion,* trans. John Allen (Philadelphia, 1838), I.xiv.xxi, I.v.xii, I.v.xi, I.vi.

vine and the branches thereof, to consider the mysticall conjunction betweene Christ and his Church: by
the sight of the rainebow to thinke of the promise of
God of not drowning the world by waters: and by
any thing that befalls, to take occasion, to consider in
it the wisdome, goodnes, justice, mercie, providence
of God, etc.[57]

According to Thomas Adams, "the very bread we eat,
should put us in mind of that bread of life; . . . the light of
the sun invites us to that everlasting light in heaven; the
winds in their airy regions, of that sacred Spirit which
blows and sanctifies where he pleaseth." John White of
Dorchester exhorts the Christian "to study Spiritual things
in the Book of Nature; and to ascend up to Heaven by
these things on Earth," but he makes it clear that man's
knowledge of the spiritual significance of earthly things is
derived from the similitudes of Christ in the Bible. One of
Christ's reasons for using similitudes in his preaching,
says White, is "that by resembling those Spirituall things
by Earthly; he might acquaint us with the right use of
those things which are subject to sense, which is to raise
up our hearts, to the contemplation of things that are
above sense." Finally Henry King states that "If the whole
World be a Booke penn'd and composed by *God:* If all
the severall sorts of Creatures be the Pages of that Booke,

57. In *Works, 1,* 647.

this *autos, He,* is the *Index* that points and directs us unto every Leafe."[58]

Orthodox meditation on the creatures differs from nature mysticism in stressing the necessity of going beyond nature to God, and the Christian reader is frequently warned not to "rest" in the creatures. Take, for example, the following passage from St. Augustine, in which the image of the shadow looks back to Plotinus and forward to Eve's description of her creation.

> Alas for those who abandon you as leader and who stray in what are but your footprints, who love the signs which you show but not yourself, who forget your meaning, O wisdom, most gracious light of a purified mind! . . . Woe to those who turn away from your light, and love to linger in their darkness! It is as if they turned their backs upon you, they are held fast in the shadow cast on them by their works of the flesh, and yet what delights them even there they still receive from the brightness shed by your light. But love of the shadow makes the soul's eye too lazy and weak to endure your sight. Then a man is wrapped more and more in darkness, while he is inclined to seek whatever his weakness can endure more easily. Gradually he is unable to see what is supreme, and to

58. Adams, *Works,* p. 175; White, *A Commentary Upon the Three First Chapters of . . . Genesis* (London, 1656), p. 45; King, *A Sermon of Deliverance. Preached . . . on Easter Monday, 1626* (London, 1626), p. 5.

think evil whatever deceives his blindness or attracts his poverty, or pains him when held captive.[59]

This theme is commonplace in the seventeenth century. William Cowper, for example, says that Adam's knowledge of God led him to the knowledge of the creature, not the other way around; fallen man, however, is "put backe, as we say, to his ABC, to learne the glory, goodnesse, and providence of the Creator, by looking to the creature." Such is our corruption, however, that we cannot even learn of God what the creatures teach us, and "wee are oftentimes so snared with the love of the creature, that wee forget the Creator."[60] John Weemse says that

> We come to the knowledge of God three manner of wayes. 1. *Per viam negationis, God is not this nor this;* Ergo, *He is this:* we proceed here, as the Carver of an Image doth, when he heweth off from the stone, this and this, to make it this. 2. *Per viam causationis,* as when we take him up by his effects. 3. *Per viam eminentiae;* what excellent things we see in the creatures, that leads us to take up what excellency is in God.
>
> This teacheth us, when we see any excellent things in the creatures, let us not rest there; but elevate our minds to the infinite beautie and greatnesse that is in God.[61]

---

59. *The Problem of Free Choice,* trans. Dom Mark Pontifex, Ancient Christian Writers, No. 22 (London, 1955), II.16.43.

60. *The Workes of Mr. William Cowper* (London, 1629), pp. 842, 404.

61. *The Christian Synagogue* (London, 1623), p. 239.

Even Henry Vaughan, whose experience of God in nature is at least closer to Wordsworth's than that of most of his contemporaries, advises us to "Search well another world; who studies this, / Travels in Clouds, seeks *Manna,* where none is." Like St. Augustine he passes "Through all the Creatures" in search of knowledge of God, but

> Since in these veyls my Ecclips'd Eye
> May not approach thee, (for at night
>
> Who can have commerce with the light?)
> I'le disapparell, and to buy
> But one half glaunce, most gladly dye.[62]

In spite of his specific references to the book of nature and the contemplation of created things, and in spite of the opportunities his subject afforded him, Milton makes very little use in *Paradise Lost* of the traditional materials associated with this theme. There is no trace of hermetic correspondences and signatures and hardly any sign of the metaphors and similes provided by the bestiaries and lapidaries, of which Du Bartas was so fond. And of course Milton's rejection of the orthodox doctrine of the Trinity made unavailable to him the wealth of analogies cherished by medieval theologians. It may be simply that Milton's taste was offended by the hackneyed and unimaginative character of much of the traditional material, but I would suggest that there are philosophical and religious as well as aesthetic reasons for his rejection of the tradition. His

---

62. "The Search" and "Vanity of Spirit."

attitude, at least at first glance, seems very close to that of Bacon and the left-wing Puritans. In the *Advancement of Learning* Bacon says that God has laid before us

> two books or volumes to study, if we will be secured from error; first, the Scriptures, revealing the Will of God; and then the creatures expressing His Power; whereof the latter is a key unto the former: not only opening our understanding to conceive the true sense of the Scriptures, by the general notions of reason and rules of speech; but chiefly opening our belief, in drawing us into a due meditation of the omnipotency of God, which is chiefly signed and engraven upon His works.

Later in Book II he says that sacred theology is not grounded upon the light of nature; the Bible says *Coeli enarrent gloriam Dei,* not *Coeli enarrent voluntatem Dei*.[63] Bacon's plea for the autonomy of scientific investigation, carefully garbed in language calculated to appeal to James I, becomes a naked severance between natural and spiritual truths in John Dury's *A Seasonable Discourse,* where "spirituall things are to be discerned spiritually, and naturall things naturally, each in his distinct, sphear and way of knowledge according to his kind."[64] Milton, I think, agreed with this general position, but he could not accept Bacon's statement that nature is the key to Scrip-

63. *The Advancement of Learning*, I.vi.16, II.xxv.3.
64. (London, 1649), p. 12.

ture, since "those written Records pure" are "not but by the Spirit understood" (XII.513–14). In fact, Milton, like most of the writers in the tradition, would put it the opposite way: Scripture is the key to a proper understanding of nature, at least in its symbolic aspect. Nature itself is witness to its inability to reveal the will of God. In the very passage in which he speaks of the Heavens as "the Book of God" Raphael warns Adam that

> God to remove his ways from human sense,
> Plac'd Heav'n from Earth so far, that earthly sight,
> If it presume, might err in things too high,
> And no advantage gain.   (VIII.119–22)

Adam, who of course knows nothing either of Scripture or of Christ, gleans from nature hardly more than the bare notion that God exists. Recounting to Raphael his experience on first awaking from creation, he says that he tried to speak and found that he could name whatever he saw.

> Thou Sun said I, fair Light,
> And thou enlight'n'd Earth, so fresh and gay,
> Ye Hills and Dales, ye Rivers, Woods, and Plains
> And ye that live and move, fair Creatures, tell,
> Tell, if ye saw, how came I thus, how here?
> Not of myself; by some great Maker then,
> In goodness and in power preeminent.
>   (VIII.273–79)

In contrast to Eve, who looks down at her shadow in the water, Adam looks upward, both literally and figuratively,

and he rises to a knowledge of the power and goodness of
his Maker, the first of Bonaventure's six steps, with wisdom
significantly omitted. When he questions the creatures,
however, he receives no answer:

> Tell me, how may I know him, how adore,
> From whom I have that thus I move and live,
> And feel that I am happier than I know.
>
> (VIII.280–82)

Lacking perforce any knowledge of the Word, Adam finds
the creatures dumb. His earthly sight may rise to the
merely natural knowledge that the universe has a Maker
but his knowledge of supernatural realities must be mediated by the ear. He is led to the Garden in a dream, and
when he wakes a "presence Divine" speaks to him. Adam,
who can name the animals because he understands their
natures, is unable to name God:

> O by what Name, for thou above all these,
> Above mankind, or aught than mankind higher,
> Surpassest far my naming, how may I
> Adore thee, Author of this Universe   (VIII.357–60)

According to Bonaventure and Hugh of St. Victor the
immensity of the world reveals the power of God the
Father, the utility of the world the goodness of God the
Holy Spirit, and the beauty of the world the wisdom of
God the Son.[65] In the lines in which he addresses the crea-
tures Adam mentions the power and goodness of God but

---

65. *On the Sacraments,* I.iii.xxviii; De Bruyne, *Études,* 2, 238.

omits wisdom, as he does in the opening lines of his morning hymn:

> These are thy glorious works, Parent of good,
> Almighty, thine this universal Frame,
> Thus wondrous fair; thyself how wondrous then!
> Unspeakable, who sit'st above these Heavens
> To us invisible or dimly seen
> In these thy lowest works, yet these declare
> Thy goodness beyond thought, and Power Divine.
>
> (V.153–59)

Although Adam again and again speaks of the creation as "fair," Milton carefully avoids the medieval equation of beauty-wisdom-Christ. One reason, no doubt, is that he did not wish to make what would appear to many of his readers to be an explicit reference to the doctrine of the Trinity. Another and perhaps more fundamental reason is that Milton regarded Christianity as a purely spiritual religion with no place for the "eye-service of the body."[66] The Garden may provide metaphors of the spiritual life which will be defined by Christ, but the literal Garden is destroyed by the Flood. The true temple is the upright heart and pure, and the fruits of the "Paradise within" are joy and eternal bliss. However much Milton may have regretted fallen man's inability to read "the Book of knowledge fair" (III.47), he nevertheless believed that "all corporeal resemblances of inward holiness and beauty are now past." For Milton, Christianity is a religion not of the eye but of the ear.

66. *Of Reformation*, *SM*, p. 441.

5

The Eye and the Ear

"Fair Eve"

The true way of going to the things of love, says Diotima
in the well-known passage from the *Symposium*,

> is to begin from the beauties of earth and mount
> upwards for the sake of that other beauty, using these
> as steps only, and from one going on to two, and from
> two to all fair forms, and from fair forms to fair
> practices, and from fair practices to fair notions,
> until from fair notions he arrives at the notion of
> absolute beauty, and at last knows what the essence
> of beauty is.[1]

Plato recognizes the beauty of the material universe—the
cosmos—but he also recognizes the need to pass beyond it
at an early stage in the ascent of the mind to the intelligible realm. This ambivalent attitude toward physical
beauty is reflected in all later Neoplatonism with varying
degrees of emphasis. Plotinus is keenly aware of "the
beauties of the realm of sense . . . that have entered into
Matter—to adorn, and to ravish, where they are seen," but
in the same sentence he calls them "images, and shadow-

---

1. *Symposium*, 211 (trans. Jowett).

pictures, fugitives." There are higher beauties, imperceptible to sense, and to contemplate these the soul must ascend toward the Good, which is the source of all beauty. "He that has the strength, let him arise and withdraw into himself, foregoing all that is known by the eyes, turning away for ever from the material beauty that once made his joy."[2]

In Renaissance Neoplatonism the emphasis shifts toward a franker delight in physical beauty, but the essentials of the Platonic ascent remain.

> The splendor of the highest Good itself shines in individual things, and where it shines more fittingly, there it especially allures him who contemplates it, excites him who looks at it, enraptures and takes possession of him who approaches it. . . . There it is apparent that the Soul is inflamed by the divine splendor, glowing in the beautiful person as in a mirror, and secretly lifted up by it as by a hook in order to become God.[3]

2. *Enneads,* I.6.3, I.6.8.

3. Ficino, *Opera omnia,* p. 306, quoted in Kristeller, *The Philosophy of Marsilio Ficino,* p. 267. Cf. Annibale Romei: "It remaineth unto me (most excellent Queen) for conclusion of this my discourse, that I declare unto your highness, that humane beuty to no other end, hath by the chiefe creator bin produced, amongst al beauties sensible, most excellent, but to kindle this honest & holy love divine, which uniteth humane creature with his creator. For man wholly astonished in beholding humane Beauty, raiseth up his mind to the contemplation of Beauty true & essential, whereof this is a shadow and similitude" *(The Courtiers Academy,* trans. J. Kepers [1598], reprinted in *The Frame of Order,* ed. James Winny

The stages by which the soul may be lifted up to God are outlined in Pico's ladder of love, which is a modification of the scheme of the *Symposium*. Here is Panofsky's summary:[4]

(1) Delight in the visible beauty of an individual (Senses).

(2) Idealization of this particular visible beauty (Imagination).

(3) Interpretation of it as a mere specimen of visible beauty in general (Reason, applied to visual experience).

(4) Interpretation of visible beauty as an expression of moral values (*'Conversione dell'anima in se,'* Reason turning away from visual experience).

(5) Interpretation of these moral values as reflexes of metaphysical ones (Reason abdicating, so to speak, in favour of the Mind).

(6) Interpretation of the metaphysical values as functions of one universal and intelligible beauty (the Human Mind uniting itself with the Cosmic Mind).

In the following passage Raphael once again appears as the spokesman for Neoplatonism, even to the point of

---

[London, George Allen & Unwin, 1957], p. 210). The appearance of this theme in medieval thought is noted by De Bruyne, *Études*, 2, 199–202.

4. Erwin Panofsky, *Studies in Iconology* (New York and Evanston, Harper Torchbooks, 1962), p. 143, n.49. See also Collins, *Christian Mysticism in the Elizabethan Age*, pp. 113–14.

limiting the contemplation of female beauty to the mind and the senses of sight and hearing and relegating the pleasures of touch to the animal level, as Ficino and Pico had done:

> But if the sense of touch whereby mankind
> Is propagated seem such dear delight
> Beyond all other, think the same voutsaf't
> To Cattle and each Beast; which would not be
> To them made common and divulg'd, if aught
> Therein enjoy'd were worthy to subdue
> The Soul of Man, or passion in him move.
> What higher in her society thou find'st
> Attractive, human, rational, love still;
> In loving thou dost well, in passion not,
> Wherein true Love consists not; Love refines
> The thoughts, and heart enlarges, hath his seat
> In Reason, and is judicious, is the scale
> By which to heav'nly Love thou may'st ascend,
> Not sunk in carnal pleasure, for which cause
> Among the Beasts no Mate for thee was found.
>
> (VIII.579–94)

This is true in an ideal Neoplatonic universe, perhaps, but in the world that Milton has created Adam's love for Eve is the scale by which he descends. In the first moments of his existence, it is true, he appears to ascend from physical beauty to intellectual beauty. In her account of her first meeting with Adam, Eve tells him how she followed a voice, addressing her as "fair Creature,"

Till I espi'd thee, fair indeed and tall,
Under a Platan, yet methought less fair,
Less winning soft, less amiably mild,
Than that smooth wat'ry image; back I turn'd,
Thou following cri'd'st aloud, Return fair *Eve,*
Whom fli'st thou? whom thou fli'st, of him thou art,
His flesh, his bone; to give thee being I lent
Out of my side to thee, nearest my heart
Substantial Life, to have thee by my side
Henceforth an individual solace dear;
Part of my Soul I seek thee, and thee claim
My other half: with that thy gentle hand
Seiz'd mine, I yielded, and from that time see
How beauty is excell'd by manly grace
And wisdom, which alone is truly fair.   (IV.477–91)

But at the crucial moment, as we shall see, Adam forgets
the lesson he has taught Eve. The fact is that Milton, in
spite of his own sensitivity to the beauties of sight and
sound, was deeply suspicious of man's response to physical
beauty, especially female beauty, and this ambivalence is
expressed in his use of the epithet "fair," which appears
five times in the passage just quoted.

"Fair" is applied several times by Adam to the works
of creation, for example, when he addresses the "fair creatures" (VIII.276) or speaks of the "universal Frame" as
"wondrous fair" in his morning hymn (V.154–55). The
word appears in an even more favorable context when the
narrator tells how the Creator returned from His work and

beheld "this new created World . . . how it show'd / In prospect from his Throne, how good, how fair, / Answering his great Idea" (VII.554–57). These same two epithets, "fair" and "good," are used by God Himself:

> See with what heat these Dogs of Hell advance
> To waste and havoc yonder World, which I
> So fair and good created   (X.616–18)

Like the physical creation of which she is both consummation and symbol, Eve too is fair, and at least nine times the word is applied to her in unambiguously favorable contexts.

But man, like Satan, "perverts best things / To worst abuse, or to thir meanest use" (IV.203–04), and the perversion soon reveals itself in language. In the following passage, which contains the first appearance of "fair" in the poem, the process of degeneration occurs in the physical, moral, and linguistic realms:

> In *Sion* also not unsung, where stood
> Her Temple on th' offensive Mountain, built
> By that uxorious King, whose heart though large,
> Beguil'd by fair Idolatresses, fell
> To Idols foul.   (I.442–46)

The descent fair-fell-foul, linguistically enacted in the regression from front to back vowels, is embodied in a visual symbol in the person of Sin, who "seem'd Woman to the waist, and fair, / But ended foul in many a scaly fold"

(II.650–51). This monstrous perversion is the issue of Satan's mind: "Hast thou forgot me then," Sin asks,

> and do I seem
> Now in thine eye so foul, once deem'd so fair
> In Heav'n, when at th' Assembly, and in sight
> Of all the Seraphim with thee combin'd
> In bold conspiracy against Heav'n's King,
> All on a sudden miserable pain
> Surpris'd thee, dim thine eyes, and dizzy swum
> In darkness, while thy head flames thick and fast
> Threw forth, till on the left side op'ning wide,
> Likest to thee in shape and count'nance bright,
> Then shining heav'nly fair, a Goddess arm'd
> Out of thy head I sprung: (II.747–58)

"Fair" might almost be called Satan's favorite word. He speaks of Death as his "fair Son" (II.818) and of Paradise as "fair" (IV.379), and he fully recognizes the dark potentialities of "fair Paradise" as he exclaims, with brilliant and diabolic irony, "O fair foundation laid whereon to build / Thir ruin!" (IV.521–22). In his soliloquy before the temptation he speaks of Eve as "divinely fair, fit Love for Gods" (IX.489), and he proceeds to address her as "Fairest resemblance of thy Maker fair" (IX.538). He uses the word eleven more times in this scene, applying it both to Eve and to the Tree of Knowledge, and he even dares to join with it God's epithet "good."

> Thenceforth to Speculations high or deep
> I turn'd my thoughts, and with capacious mind

> Consider'd all things visible in Heav'n,
> Or Earth, or Middle, all things fair and good;
> But all that fair and good in thy Divine
> Semblance, and in thy Beauty's heav'nly Ray
> United I beheld; no Fair to thine
> Equivalent or second   (IX.602–09)

Having learned from Adam that manly grace and wisdom alone are "truly fair," Eve should have recognized Satan's perversion of values in his insistence on the literal meaning of the word. One can hardly blame her, however, since she is all but identified with the physical level of existence and the whole tendency of her mind is to "rest in the creatures." In contrast to Adam, whose first act is to turn his eyes and mind toward Heaven, Eve instinctively looks down at her "smooth wat'ry image" (IV.480), and to her the "clear / Smooth Lake" seems "another Sky" (IV.458–59). A similar contrast between Adam and Eve may be seen when Raphael visits the Garden. Eve says she

> will haste and from each bough and brake,
> Each Plant and juiciest Gourd will pluck such choice
> To entertain our Angel guest, as hee
> Beholding shall confess that here on Earth
> God hath dispenst his bounties as in Heav'n.
>   (V.326–30)

But Adam realizes there is a better food. "For while I sit with thee," he says to Raphael,

> I seem in Heav'n,
> And sweeter thy discourse is to my ear

Than Fruits of Palm-tree pleasantest to thirst
And hunger both, from labor, at the hour
Of sweet repast; they satiate, and soon fill,
Though pleasant, but thy words with Grace Divine
Imbu'd, bring to thir sweetness no satiety.
                                        (VIII.210–16)

It is not surprising, then, that Satan should succeed in convincing Eve that the literal fruit has spiritual properties. One might say, in fact, that she has been trapped by the fallacy of the "sacred metaphor."[5] Lamenting her ignorance of good and evil she says,

Here grows the Cure of all, this Fruit Divine,
Fair to the Eye, inviting to the Taste,
Of virtue to make wise: what hinders then
To reach, and feed at once both Body and Mind?
                                        (IX.776–79)

Adam has no excuse, however, for he is well aware of the danger of taking the word "fair" in too literal a sense. In lecturing Eve on the psychology of temptation (Adam's sentiments are irreproachable when he lectures Eve) he says,

But God left free the Will, for what obeys
Reason, is free, and Reason he made right,
But bid her well beware, and still erect,

5. See Chap. 3, above.

> Lest by some fair appearing good surpris'd
> She dictate false, and misinform the Will
>
> (IX.351–55)

Raphael tries to warn Adam that the "fair appearing good" might be Eve herself:

> For what admir'st thou, what transports thee so,
> An outside? fair no doubt, and worthy well
> Thy cherishing, thy honoring, and thy love,
> Not thy subjection: weigh with her thyself;
> Then value: (VIII.567–71)

But manly grace and wisdom are forgotten when Eve approaches with "A bough of fairest fruit that downy smil'd" (IX.851). "O fairest of Creation," Adam exclaims to himself, echoing the language of Satan,

> O fairest of Creation, last and best
> Of all God's Works, Creature in whom excell'd
> Whatever can to sight or thought be form'd,
> Holy, divine, good, amiable, or sweet! (IX.896–99)

Eve may be fairest to sight, but not to thought. The contemplation of visual beauty, it would seem, is not the first step in the ascent to God. Adam eats of the "fair enticing Fruit" (IX.996), and the result is a darkening of his intellectual vision that manifests itself immediately in a degradation of language:

> But come, so well refresh't, now let us play,
> As meet is, after such delicious Fare;

For never did thy Beauty since the day
I saw thee first and wedded thee, adorn'd
With all perfections, so inflame my sense
With ardor to enjoy thee, fairer now
Than ever, bounty of this virtuous Tree.

(IX.1027–33)

"Fair Eve," the physical glory of God's "fair Paradise,"
has become a "fair Idolatress." Adam, beguiled, has fallen
to idols foul, and he now sees Eve as "fairer" than she was
when he thought of her as "fairest of Creation." In the
alembic of the mind—Adam's or Satan's—the physical
universe is transformed, and what began as "fair and
good" ends "foul in many a scaly fold" (II.651). Having
closed his ear to "The high Injunction not to taste that
Fruit" (X.13), Adam submits his reason to the evidence of
his eye, which Donne called "the devils doore."

"Close at the ear of Eve"

It is a commonplace of intellectual history that sight is
the noblest of the senses,[6] and it is not surprising that when

6. Plato, *Republic*, VI.507; E. V. Arnold, *Roman Stoicism* (Cambridge,
Cambridge University Press, 1911), p. 130; Horace, *Ars Poetica*, vv. 180–82;
St. Augustine, *De Trinitate*, XI.i.i; De Bruyne, *Études*, 2, 245–46; John
Donne, "Sermon Preached at St. Paul's, on Easter Day, 1628," in *The
Sermons of John Donne*, ed. Evelyn M. Simpson and George R. Potter, *8*
(Berkeley and Los Angeles, 1956), 221; George Herbert, *Works*, ed. F. C.
Hutchinson (Oxford, Clarendon Press, 1941), p. 201; Sibbes, *Works, 4*,
250–51. See also Jean H. Hagstrum, *The Sister Arts* (Chicago, 1958),
pp. 3–13.

Christian writers wished to distinguish spiritual from sense knowledge they spoke metaphorically of the eye of the soul, as St. Bonaventure does when he says that man has a triple eye, "the eye of the flesh by which he sees the world and those things that are in the world, the eye of reason by which he sees the soul and those things that are in the soul, the eye of contemplation by which he sees God and those things that are in God." According to Hugh of St. Victor, from whom St. Bonaventure apparently derived his doctrine of the triple eye, Adam was endowed with an eye of the flesh which was not blinded by the Fall, an eye of reason which was clouded by the Fall, and an eye of contemplation which was completely extinguished by the Fall.[7]

In an interesting article A. B. Chambers[8] has recently suggested that this doctrine of the inner eye lies behind the prologue to Book III of *Paradise Lost:*

> Thus with the Year
> Seasons return, but not to me returns
> Day, or the sweet approach of Ev'n or Morn,
> Or sight of vernal bloom, or Summer's Rose,
> Or flocks, or herds, or human face divine;
> But cloud instead, and ever-during dark
> Surrounds me, from the cheerful ways of men
> Cut off, and for the Book of knowledge fair

7. *Breviloquium,* II.12.5; *On the Sacraments,* I.x.ii.
8. "Wisdom at One Entrance Quite Shut Out: *Paradise Lost,* III, 1–55," *PQ, 42* (1963), 114–19.

Presented with a Universal blanc
Of Nature's works to me expung'd and ras'd,
And wisdom at one entrance quite shut out.
So much the rather thou Celestial Light
Shine inward, and the mind through all her powers
Irradiate, there plant eyes, all mist from thence
Purge and disperse, that I may see and tell
Of things invisible to mortal sight.   (III.40–55)

Chambers links the mist that Milton asks God to "purge and disperse" to the darkening of Adam's mind after the Fall: "Soon found thir Eyes how op'n'd, and thir minds / How dark'n'd" (IX.1053–54). In point of fact, however, Milton did not endow Adam with an eye of contemplation by which he might see things invisible to mortal sight. Adam sees only the physical universe, and he proclaims in his morning hymn that in His works God is "invisible" or but "dimly seen" (V.157).[9] On the ladder of contemplation Adam rises by an elementary act of logical deduction only to the bare knowledge of a good and powerful Maker. Like most Protestants Milton rejected altogether the favorite idea of medieval mysticism that man may find God by turning inward and ascending to the "apex mentis."[10] In the lines quoted above Milton does not merely pray that God disperse the mists that have darkened his mind; he also asks God to plant eyes that can see things invisible to

9. Cf. John Weemse: "So the Lord preacheth indistinctly (as it were) by his worke; but by the sound of his Gospel, hee preacheth clearely and plainely" (*Exercitations*, Ep. Ded.).

10. J. S. Whale, *The Protestant Tradition* (Cambridge, 1955), pp. 26–31.

157

mortal sight. In the prologue to Book IX we learn that the seeds of spiritual vision are planted through the ear:

> Mee of these
> Nor skill'd nor studious, higher Argument
> Remains, sufficient of itself to raise
> That name, unless an age too late, or cold
> Climate, or Years damp my intended wing
> Deprest; and much they may, if all be mine,
> Not Hers who brings it nightly to my Ear.
>
> (IX.41–47)

As Richard Sibbes said, "Hearing begets seeing in religion."[11] For Milton, as for Adam, supernatural knowledge is mediated by the word.

Christianity, as Amos Wilder recently pointed out, is primarily a religion of the ear.[12] St. Paul said that "Faith is by hearing" and that "we walk by faith, and not by sight,"[13] and his words echo through the Christian centuries, most resonantly perhaps in the early Middle Ages and during the Reformation. Testimony from secular thought is not lacking. Even Plato, for whom sight was the noblest sense, considered the visual arts inferior to the arts of language and the written word inferior to the spoken word.[14] According to Theophrastus the ear is superior to

11. In *Works, 4,* 252. This statement occurs in a discussion of the spiritual eye.

12. *The Language of the Gospel: Early Christian Rhetoric* (New York, 1964), pp. 14–20.

13. Rom. 10:17; II Cor. 5:7.

14. *Statesman,* 277; *Phaedrus,* 278.

the eye, and he is followed by Boethius. In the earlier Middle Ages the classical witness is confirmed by the Pauline dictum, as exemplified in Bernard of Silvester and Alan of Lille. In the high Middle Ages the eye regains its favored position in the natural hierarchy. Hugh of St. Victor regards the eye as superior to the ear because things, which are created by God, are superior to words, created by man. But he also says that it is more meritorious to have faith by hearing than knowledge by sight.[15] In the Reformation, as might be expected, the emphasis falls very heavily on the superiority of hearing. Donne and Vaughan are perhaps the most eloquent witnesses:

> Man hath a natural way to come to God, by the eie, by the creature; So *Visible things* shew the *Invisible God:* But then, God hath super-induced a supernaturall way, by the eare. For, though hearing be naturall, yet that faith in God should come by hearing a man preach, is supernatural. God shut up the naturall way, in *Saul*, Seeing; He struck him blind; But he opened the super-naturall way, he inabled him to heare, and to heare him.[16]

15. De Bruyne, *Études, 1,* 11; *2,* 89–90, 245–46. Cf. Aquinas, *S.T.,* III, Q. 12, Art. 3, ad 2. Hugh of St. Victor, *On the Sacraments,* I.x.ii.

16. John Donne, "Sermon Preached at St. Paul's, the Sunday After the Conversion of St. Paul, 1624 [1624/5]," in *The Sermons of John Donne, 6,* 217. There is an informative discussion of the Puritan emphasis on preaching (as against reading) in Lawrence A. Sasek, *The Literary Temper of the English Puritans* (Baton Rouge, 1961), Chap. 2, and U. Milo Kaufmann has some suggestive remarks on the Puritan preference for logos over

Why with so much dotage do we fixe our Eyes upon the deceitfull lookes of temporal things? Why do we rest our selves upon those thornes onely, which wee see beneath us? Is it the Eye alone that wee live by? Is there nothing usefull about us but that wanderer? We live also by the eare, and at that Inlet wee receive the glad tydings of Salvation.[17]

The religious emphasis on the superiority of the ear may be seen in another context if we recall that it was a commonplace of the poetry of the *dolce stil novo* that love strikes the heart through the eye. Examples abound in Mott's *The System of Courtly Love,*[18] but Chaucer's Palamon tells us all we have to know:

> This prison caused me nat for to crye,
> But I was hurt right now thurghout myn ye
> Into myn herte, that wol my bane be.
> The fairnesse of that lady that I see
> Yond in the gardyn romen to and fro
> Is cause of al my criyng and my wo.[19]

---

mythos in *The Pilgrim's Progress and Traditions in Puritan Meditation,* Chap. 2.

17. Henry Vaughan, *The World Contemned,* in *Works,* ed. L. C. Martin (2 vols. Oxford, Clarendon Press, 1914), *1,* 326.

18. (Boston and London, 1896), esp. pp. 19–20, 50, 68–70, 85, 113, 121, 122. The *locus classicus* is *Phaedrus,* 251.

19. *Knight's Tale,* I.1095–1100, *The Complete Works of Chaucer,* ed. Fred N. Robinson (Cambridge, Mass., 1933).

Even in secular love poetry, however, the ear begins to assert its claim to be the organ of understanding, and in his romantic comedies Shakespeare quite consistently relegates the eye to a lower rung on the hierarchy of the senses. Bassanio, for example, is warned that fancy, not love, is bred in the eyes, and Claudio can win Hero only when he agrees to take her sight unseen. Marvell, in whose poetry so many intellectual currents find limpid and graceful statement, sums it all up in the first stanza of "The Fair Singer."

> To make a final conquest of all me,
> Love did compose so sweet an Enemy,
> In whom both Beauties to my death agree,
> Joyning themselves in fatal Harmony;
> That while she with her Eyes my Heart does bind,
> She with her Voice might captivate my Mind.

All of these traditions, both secular and religious, are subtly interwoven in the work of George Herbert. Although he accepts the classic dictum that the eye is the noblest of the senses, he warns his parson to choose a wife not by his eye but by his ear, and he tells his parishioners to shut up their eyes at service, since all comes in by the ear.[20] In the lyric poetry of *The Temple* God "eyes" the heart, just as courtly lovers do, but man's eyes "feed on earth" and are blinded by dust, and they must be

20. In *Works*, pp. 201, 238, 23.

"mended" by Holy Scripture before man can attain spiritual vision.[21]

In the devotional literature and sermons of the seventeenth century the eye is associated particularly with Satan. John Donne (who may have known what he was talking about) said that "The eye is the devils doore, before the eare: for, though he doe enter at the eare, by wanton discourse, yet he was at the eye before; we see, before we talke dangerously. But the eare is the Holy Ghosts first doore."[22] Richard Brathwaite thought that "there is no passage more easie for the entry of vice, than by the crany of the eye; there she hath first acceptance, facilest entrance, and assuredst continuance."[23] Donne and Brathwaite are speaking of fallen man; Adam and Eve, however, according to Richard Sibbes and William Cowper, were attacked by the Devil not through the eye but through the ear:

> Death came in by the ear at the first. Adam hearing the serpent, that he should not have heard, death came in by the ear.

> The first Sense by regeneration restored to the children of God, is the sense of Hearing. As the eare was the first port by which death was convayed to the soule; so is it the first by which life enters into it. *Evah* by hearing what the Serpent said, was brought to a

21. "Mattens," "The Dawning," "Frailtie," "The H. Scriptures I."

22. "Sermon Preached at St. Paul's, on Easter Day, 1628," in *The Sermons of John Donne, 8,* 228.

23. *Essayes upon the Five Senses* (2d ed. London, 1635), p. 3.

delectation in sinne: and the Christian by hearing
what the Spirit saith, is brought to a confident hatred
of sinne.[24]

In the temptation scene in *Paradise Lost* both the eye
and the ear come under attack. Eve, whose understanding
is more vulnerable than Adam's, is assaulted chiefly
through the ear, though all of her senses are involved:

> He ended, and his words replete with guile
> Into her heart too easy entrance won:
> Fixt on the Fruit she gaz'd, which to behold
> Might tempt alone, and in her ears the sound
> Yet rung of his persuasive words, impregn'd
> With Reason, to her seeming, and with Truth;
> Meanwhile the hour of Noon drew on, and wak'd
> An eager appetite, rais'd by the smell
> So savory of that Fruit, which with desire,
> Inclinable now grown to touch or taste,
> Solicited her longing eye   (IX.733–43)

For Adam, who sinned against his better knowledge, the
fatal entrance is through the eye:

> O fairest of Creation, last and best
> Of all God's Works, Creature in whom excell'd
> Whatever can to sight or thought be form'd
> (IX.896–98)

24. Sibbes, *Works, 4,* 252; *The Anatomy of a Christian-Man,* in *The
Workes of Mr. William Cowper,* p. 291.

The first result of their sin is the opening of their eyes to the entrance of lust:

> but that false Fruit
> Far other operation first display'd,
> Carnal desire inflaming, hee on *Eve*
> Began to cast lascivious Eyes, she him
> As wantonly repaid; in Lust they burn
>
> (IX.1011–15)

Eve's "Eye dart[s] cantagious Fire" as Adam exhibits that his command of metaphorical language can be used to degrade as well as enhance:

> *Eve,* now I see thou are exact of taste,
> And elegant, of Sapience no small part,
> Since to each meaning savor we apply,
> And Palate call judicious   (IX.1017–20)

Adam has come a long way since he told Raphael "sweeter thy discourse is to my ear / Than Fruits of Palm-tree pleasantest to thirst / And hunger both" (VIII.211–13).

Eve's temptation begins when Satan, "Squat like a Toad, close at the ear of *Eve*" (IV.800), whispers to her the language of courtly love, and Adam's begins when he first sees Eve and realizes that he is weak "Against the charm of Beauty's powerful glance" (VIII.533). With his eyes full of Eve's physical beauty, Adam closes his ear to God's "high Injunction not to taste that Fruit" (X.13) and hearkens to the voice of his wife (X.198). "The voice of God" (X.97), which Adam "oft [had] heard, and [had] not fear'd" (X.119), now becomes terrible to him: "I heard thee in the Garden, and of thy voice / Afraid, being naked, hid myself" (X.116–17). When Christ judges him, then, it is for his failure in hearing: "Was shee thy God, that her thou didst obey / Before his voice" (X.145–46).

As expected, Adam's regeneration is accomplished chiefly through the ear, and the decisive upward movement begins when he considers the significance of Christ's metaphorical prophecy:

> Then let us seek
> Some safer resolution, which methinks
> I have in view, calling to mind with heed
> Part of our Sentence, that thy Seed shall bruise
> The Serpent's head; piteous amends, unless
> Be meant, whom I conjecture, our grand Foe
> *Satan,* who in the Serpent hath contriv'd
> Against us this deceit: to crush his head
> Would be revenge indeed   (X.1028–36)

Adam, in whose mind the seeds of grace have already been planted, understands the metaphor, while Satan does not:

> True is, mee also he hath judg'd, or rather
> Mee not, but the brute Serpent in whose shape
> Man I deceiv'd: that which to mee belongs,
> Is enmity, which he will put between
> Mee and Mankind; I am to bruise his heel;
> His Seed, when is not set, shall bruise my head:
> A World who would not purchase with a bruise,
> Or much more grievous pain?   (X.494–501)

In the last two books, as Barbara Lewalski has amply demonstrated, "Adam's shift from vision to non-vision is related to a pervasive pattern of sight imagery throughout the prophecy," a pattern which develops St. Paul's dictum that "we walk by faith, not by sight." "Adam's spiritual vision grows keener as his physical sight declines,"[25] until finally he attains "the sum / Of wisdom" by acknowledging as his Redeemer Christ, Whose voice he has heard, but Whose flesh he has never seen.

Word and Image

The emphasis of Reformation Protestantism on the preaching of the Word and its rejection of the *visibilia* of traditional Christian worship have led many critics to assume that a Puritan who rejects sensuous appeals in religious worship—music, bodily gesture, symbolic garments, pictures, and images—is somehow committed to denuding his poetry of imagery, whether or not he in fact succeeded. As early as 1895 Sir John Seeley wondered at the "strange inconsistency" of *Paradise Lost.*

> A Puritan has rebelled against sensuous worship. He has risen in indignation against a scheme of religion which was too material, too sensuous, which degraded invisible and awful realities by too near an association with what was visible and familiar. But in the mean-

25. "Structure and the Symbolism of Vision in Michael's Prophecy, *Paradise Lost,* Books XI–XII," *PQ, 42* (1963), 25–35.

while a poet, who is the same person, having a mind inveterately plastic and creative, is quite unable to think, even on religious subjects, without forms distinctly conceived. And, therefore, while with one hand he throws down forms, with the other he raises them up. The iconoclast is at the same time an idolater.[26]

Dowden's answer to this criticism of *Paradise Lost*—that Milton was an iconoclast only of those sensuous forms which were the growth of human tradition and that his "mythology" was not Greek but exclusively scriptural—is only partially true and partially relevant, and Seeley's words have found many echoes in more recent criticism. Professor Wolfe, for example, finds

> a striking contradiction between Milton the poet and Milton the religious thinker. As a poet Milton was constantly aware of the need of images, of dependence upon the magic of color and sound and touch, of the efficacy of pageantry and music to release the inmost springs of his reader's mind. Master of the classicist art, he understood how to transport his readers into the realm of fantasy through the medium of sensory language. Yet in religious practices he rejected the uses of art.[27]

26. Quoted in Edward Dowden, *Puritan and Anglican* (London, 1900), p. 176.

27. Don Wolfe, ed., *Complete Prose Works of John Milton* (New Haven, Yale University Press, 1953–), *1*, 109.

In fact, Milton cannot be considered a Puritan at all if we accept Patrick Cruttwell's statement that the Puritan is "by nature comparatively un-sensuous."

> When a poet like Donne or Herbert or Vaughan—and a dramatist like Shakespeare or Tourneur—expresses an ascetic revulsion from and rejection of the sensuous, their asceticism seems to express itself, paradoxically, in thoroughly sensuous terms, so that the physical world has returned, as it were, by a back-door. . . . With the real Puritan, on the other hand, the rejection seems complete. There is with him no return of the sensuous, and the final result is an art permanently impoverished in that respect, rendered barer and more abstract. The difference can be seen more clearly in the visual arts. . . . Since [the Puritan] is by nature comparatively un-sensuous, ideas are in him farther away from sensations than they are in such men as Donne and Shakespeare and the society in which they wrote; his mind is in consequence simpler.[28]

One wonders who these "real" Puritans of Cruttwell's might be—surely not the Bunyan of *Grace Abounding,* for whom ideas were often quite literally sensations.

Kenneth Murdock begins his classic study of *Literature & Theology in Colonial New England* by establishing an opposition between "the Catholic and the Protestant

28. *The Shakespearean Moment* (New York, Modern Library Paperbacks, 1960), pp. 140–41.

attitudes toward the senses, toward material objects which appeal strongly to them, and toward the use of such objects in worship."[29] "Most critics agree," he says, "that strict English Protestantism—especially in its severer varieties—tends to distrust the senses and so to offer scantier materials for art than the tradition of Rome." According to this view, Anglican writers of the earlier seventeenth century strike a happy medium between the un-English sensuous luxuriance of a "typical" Catholic poet such as Crashaw and the bare, abstract, ratiocinative style of a "typical" (though unnamed) Puritan. "A 'middle attitude,'" Murdock goes on to say, "rejecting the too expansively sensuous or even sensual quality of much Catholic art and avoiding also the extreme Protestant distrust of all that appeals to the senses, is the sign manual of the great Anglican religious literature of the seventeenth century."[30]

Like light in the Neoplatonic system of emanations, however, the clarity of these concepts becomes darker and darker the closer one approaches the realm of concrete works of art. Crashaw serves admirably as an example of a certain kind of Catholic art, but what about the great body of dull, plain-style Anglican sermons of which W. Fraser Mitchell speaks?[31] What does one do with Bunyan and Milton? What would happen to this neat system of categories if, instead of opposing the great literary artists of Anglicanism

29. (Cambridge, Mass., 1959), p. 8.
30. Ibid., pp. 17, 26.
31. *English Pulpit Oratory* (London, 1932), p. 368.

to the mass of mediocre Puritans, one opposed the great literary artists of Puritanism to the mass of mediocre Anglicans? What if the imaginative richness of Thomas Adams were set against Joseph Hall's Senecanism (and Hall is far from being a mediocre Anglican) or the poetry of Milton and Marvell against the devotional poetry in Edward Farr's anthology?[32] Without descending at all from the height of the Anglican achievement one is certainly entitled to ask whether Donne's poetry is more sensuous—in any sense of the word—than Milton's or Spenser's. Even in the more abstract religious context from which Murdock's categories derive, a moment's reflection on the controversy between St. Bernard and Abbot Suger regarding the use of the senses in worship, or on the style of Thomas Aquinas, or on St. John of the Cross' depreciatory view of images and ceremonies might suggest that what we have to deal with is not an essential difference between Catholics and Protestants but rather a difference in psychological types.[33]

Instead of revising their concepts in the light of these facts, however, critics perform feats of verbal legerdemain

32. *Select Poetry Chiefly Devotional of the Reign of Queen Elizabeth*, ed. Edward Farr (Cambridge, Parker Society, 1845).

33. Erwin Panofsky, *Meaning in the Visual Arts* (New York, 1955), pp. 108–45 on Abbot Suger and St. Bernard; M.-D. Chenu, *Introduction à l'étude de Saint Thomas D'Aquin* (Montreal, 1950), pp. 92–94, 144–46 on the style of Aquinas; St. John of the Cross, *Ascent of Mount Carmel*, Bk. III, Chaps. 35–36. Etienne Gilson points out that "in spite of all his formidable asceticism St. Bernard was no puritan when it came to literature. The Walls of his monasteries were bare, but his style was not bare" (*The Mystical Theology of St. Bernard* [London and New York, 1940], p. 63).

until the facts illustrate the concepts. Thus Donne was not popular among the Puritans because "his religious poems were too sensuously conceived," whereas Herbert was popular because "the central note of his work was the emotion of an individual believer" and his imagery, though "often drawn from Anglican forms and practices," was, "compared to Donne's, restrained, and there are few of his lines that even a strict Puritan could consider dangerous in their appeal to man's vagrant passions."[34] One would have thought that "the emotion of an individual believer" was more central to Donne's religious poetry than to Herbert's and that Donne would therefore have a stronger appeal for Puritans. But "his religious poems were too sensuously conceived," and sensuous imagery, it would appear, is more un-Puritanical than imagery "drawn from Anglican forms and practices."

As Herbert is thus pushed toward the Puritan end of the spectrum, so Edward Taylor gets pushed even further in the other direction. Taylor's "consistent selection of the Biblical imagery richest in color and in sensuous or even erotic effect, and his use in the 'Meditations' of the Song of Solomon more often than any other book of the Bible, suggest that as a poet he unconsciously moved away from the relative asceticism of the Puritan toward the Catholic acceptance of the role of the senses in worship."[35] By this time the terms "Puritan" and "Catholic," which

34. Murdock, pp. 153–54.
35. Ibid., pp. 169–70.

began as religious concepts, have become purely literary in reference; the appearances have been saved and the conceptual system, by means of a semantic shuffle, has been preserved in all its Platonic splendor. We might well complain with the Puritan John Weemse that "since the fall men impose wrong names to things, as they call light darknesse, and darknesse light."[36]

The whole of this critical structure rests on a very insecure foundation, namely the assumption that images in worship and imagery in poetry are the same kind of thing. Is this a self-evident truth? Does renunciation of the one logically commit the Puritan poet to renunciation of the other? Or, to put the question another way, does acceptance of imagery in literature imply acceptance of images in worship?

There were those in the seventeenth century who thought so or at least professed to think so for the purposes of controversy, but they were not Puritans. Catholic apologists argued that reading a description in the Bible did not differ in kind from seeing a picture of the person or event described. Nicholas Sander, for example, said that he saw no reason why "that may not be painted before our eyes, which may be preached to our eares. Againe, seing he that can reade the holie Scriptures, must needes find the said visions in the Bible: why may not he as well see on the Church wall, as in white paper, speciallie seing moe can understand the meaning of an Image, then can reade

36. *Exercitations*, p. 30. Cf. Isa. 5:20.

and understand the Bible."[37] Sander goes even further, claiming with the Florentine Neoplatonists[38] that

> the eye being the highest & most spirituall outward sense, is moe ready to instruct the mind after that sort, as it apprehendeth every thing. By which meanes we are come to the case, that the painted Image is an easier and a more lively way to instruct us, then any Oratour: and thereby it deserveth also more honour, then any Oratour, in so much that we say of him who can tell his tale most lively, that he seemed to paint it forth, and to doe it, rather then to speake and report it.[39]

The obverse of these arguments is presented by John Smyth, a Brownist who separated from the congregation at Amsterdam and established a conventicle at Leyden.

37. *A Treatise of the Images of Christ, and of His Saints* (S. Omers, 1624), p. 100.

38. See E. H. Gombrich, "The Visual Image in Neo-Platonic Thought," *Journal of the Warburg and Courtauld Institutes, 11* (1948), 163–92, and the introduction to *The Hieroglyphics of Horapollo,* trans. George Boas, Bollingen Series, *23* (New York, 1950), pp. 21–24. Edgar Wind maintains (contra Gombrich) that Ficino systematically placed the visual medium below the verbal *(Pagan Mysteries in the Renaissance* [New Haven, 1958], p. 110).

39. *A Treatise of the Images of Christ,* pp. 161–62. Cf. Plato's assertion of the primacy of the word in *Statesman,* 277 (trans. Jowett): "And our discussion might be compared to a picture of some living being which had been fairly drawn in outline, but had not yet attained the life and clearness which is given by the blending of colours. Now to intelligent persons a living being had better be delineated by language and discourse than by any painting or work of art: to the duller sort by works of art."

"Bookes or writings," he says, "are signes or pictures of things signified therby. . . . Hence it followeth that bookes or writinges are in the nature of pictures or Images & therefore in the nature of ceremonies: & so by consequent reading a booke is ceremoniall."[40] This identification of books with images was challenged by Henry Ainsworth, who was teacher of the church in Amsterdam from which Smyth broke off. "If M. Sm. can prove *books* & *images* to be both of a nature, & both alike ceremonies: he may be a Proctour for the Pope, who hath brought *images* into the Church, for *laie mens* books." But there is no likeness, for "an image when it is looked upon, affoardeth a man no edification (no not if it were an image sent from heaven, unlesse it had a *voice* withall:) but a book when it is read, informeth the mind, and feedeth not the eye onely, as dooth a picture."[41]

Ainsworth's view was the one adopted by most seventeenth-century Puritans. Indeed, it had the sanction of Calvin, who everywhere asserts the primacy of the word. Even under the old dispensation with its external symbols and ceremonies, he says, God always accompanied His revelations with a word. "Whenever God offered any sign to the holy Patriarchs it was inseparably attached to doctrine without which our senses would gaze bewildered

40. *The Differences of the Churches of the Separation* (1608), in *Works*, ed. W. T. Whitley (Cambridge, 1915), *1*, 278–79.

41. *A Defence of the Holy Scriptures, Worship, and Ministerie . . .* (Amsterdam, 1609), pp. 22–23. Cf. Ben Jonson's remarks on the superiority of poetry to painting in *Timber* and the Preface to *Hymenaei*.

upon an unmeaning object."[42] Commenting on Exodus 33:19 he says, "Figures are illusory without an explanation." Thus in speaking of the two Christian sacraments, Calvin says that their chief part consists in the word; without it "they will be, as it were, dead images."[43] But Calvin does not go on to draw the conclusion of modern critics. If he does not allow the use of man-made images and ceremonies (the earthly elements of the two sacraments were of course ordained by God), he does not therefore insist that sermons be written in a bare and abstract style. On the contrary, he says that if the Word is truly preached, men will both see and feel the truth of Christ crucified more deeply than by looking at a "thousand crosses of wood and stone."

> Let those who would discharge aright the ministry of the Gospel learn not merely to speak or to declaim, but to penetrate the consciences of men, and make them see Christ crucified, and feel the shedding of His blood. When the Church has painters such as these, she no longer needs the dead images of wood and stone, she no longer requires pictures; both of which unquestionably were first admitted to Christian temples when the pastors had become dumb and been converted into mere idols, or when they uttered a

42. *Institutes*, IV.xiv.iv, cited in Ronald S. Wallace, *Calvin's Doctrine of the Word and Sacrament* (Edinburgh, 1953), p. 72.

43. Wallace, pp. 72, 73. Aquinas says that the sacraments have a certain conformity to Christ "in that the word is joined to the sensible sign, just as in the mystery of the Incarnation the Word of God is united to sensible flesh" *(S.T.*, III, Q. 60, Art. 6).

few words from a pulpit in such a cold and careless manner that the power and efficacy of the ministry were utterly extinguished.[44]

This exhortation to imaginative preaching by the arch-logician of the Reformation finds a response in the actual sermon literature of sixteenth- and seventeenth-century Puritanism,[45] and it is echoed by the great Puritan theologians William Perkins and Richard Baxter. Perkins says that in order truly to know Christ crucified you must

> behold him often, not in the wooden crucifix after the Popish manner, but in the preaching of the word, and in the Sacraments, in which thou shalt see *him crucified* before thine eies, Gal. 3.1. Desire not here upon earth to behold him with the bodily eie but looke upon him with the eie of truth and lively faith, applying him and his merits to thy selfe as thine owne, and that with broken and bruised heart, as the poor Israelites stung with fierie serpents even to death, beheld the brasen serpent.[46]

The following passage from Baxter's *The Saints Everlasting Rest* contains the same condemnation of physical

---

44. Commentary on Gal. 3:1, cited in Wallace, pp. 248–49. Cf. *Institutes,* I.xi.vii. Cf. also the claim in Sylvester's *Du Bartas* that poetry is "a Learned Table, giving / To spirituall eyes, not painted *Christ,* but living" *(Works,* ed. Grosart, p. 222 [Second Week, Fourth Day, First Book, vv. 1018–19]).

45. William Haller, *The Rise of Puritanism* (New York, 1938), Chap. 4.

46. *A Declaration of the True Manner of Knowing Christ Crucified,* in *Works* (Cambridge, 1603), p. 758.

images and the same exaltation of the imagination as found in Calvin, Perkins, and Milton:

> Suppose, therefore, with thyself thou hadst been that apostle's fellow-traveller into the celestial kingdom, and that thou hadst seen all the saints in their white robes, with palms in their hand; suppose thou hadst heard those songs of Moses and of the Lamb; or didst even now hear them praising and glorifying the living God. If thou hadst seen these things, indeed, in what a rapture wouldst thou have been! And the more seriously thou puttest this supposition to thyself, the more will the meditation elevate thy heart. I would not have thee, as the papists, draw them in pictures, nor use such ways to represent them. This, as it is a course forbidden by God, so it would but seduce and draw down thy heart; but get the liveliest picture of them in thy mind that possibly thou canst; meditate of them as if thou wert all the while beholding them.[47]

Finally, into this context may be drawn the passage, already quoted, in which Tyndale contends that although we can prove nothing with Old Testament ceremonies,

> yet when we have once found out Christ and his mysteries, then we may borrow figures, that is to say allegories, similitudes, or examples to open Christ, and the secrets of God hid in Christ, even unto the

47. (London, 1650), p. 220.

quick, and to declare them more lively and sensibly
with them than with all the words of the world. For
similitudes have more virtue and power with them
than bare words, and lead a man's wits farther into
the pith and marrow and spiritual understanding of
the thing than all the words that can be imagined.[48]

Tyndale here claims for verbal images drawn from the
Old Testament the same function and the same superiority
over "bare words" that contemporary Catholics claimed
for visual images. We have already noted Nicholas Sander's
contention that "the painted Image is an easier and a more
lively way to instruct us, then any Oratour," and we may
add Hugh Cressy's argument that the "true inward sence"
of the doctrines of Christ's death for man and the Real
Presence in the Eucharist are "conveyed more intelligibly,
and repraesented more exactly, lively and naturally by
such practises and solemne spectacles, then by bare wordes,
though they had beene never so cleare, and of never soe
studied a perspicuity."[49] For Catholics like Sander and
Cressy (whose views, incidentally, Thomas Aquinas would
not have approved of)[50] the Word has apparently become
flesh only to remain flesh. For Milton and for Puritans in
general the flesh remains only in the word. It is Christ
alone Who gives significance to the "shadowy Types" of
the Old Testament, just as words alone give significance to

48. *A Prologue into . . . Leviticus*, in *Works, 1*, 28.
49. *Exomologesis* (Paris, 1647), p. 181.
50. *S.T.*, III, Q. 60, Art. 4, ad 2; Art. 6.

physical objects. But the Word of Christ penetrates men's hearts not by "bare words" and abstract ideas but only by "lively images" drawn from the very types that had been abolished by Christ's coming and from the symbolic language used by the Holy Spirit in the Bible. Milton's Christ is not a "bare word," not the abstract logos of the classical philosophers, for although He is the Word by which we hear God, He is also the "image, as it were [Milton's qualifying phrase is important], by which we see God."[51] The word of classical philosophy was made flesh in order that the flesh might be made Word for Christians, that is, in order that the partial images and "shadowy Types" of Christ scattered throughout human history, and especially the history of the Chosen People, might be molded "into an immortal feature of loveliness and perfection," in order that the "unmeaning objects" upon which our senses gaze bewildered might be given the radiance of intelligibility through the mediation of language.

Without pressing the analogy too far, one might say that Milton has telescoped Joachim of Floris' age of the Son and age of the Spirit. According to Joachim, the age of the Son (which was to end in 1260 A.D.) is an intermediary period between the Letter and the Spirit; it is the age of study and wisdom, the age of reading, the age of the Word. With the coming of the age of the Spirit all such verbal mediations, along with the ecclesiastical hierarchy and the sacraments, will be abolished and the church will

51. *Christian Doctrine*, I.vi, *SM*, p. 973.

be purified; *significantia* will pass over to *significata*. For Milton this passage has already been made in the ascent

> From shadowy Types to Truth, from Flesh to Spirit,
> From imposition of strict Laws, to free
> Acceptance of large Grace, from servile fear
> To filial, works of Law to works of Faith.   (XII.303–06)

But although the physical mediations have been abolished, the word and the image remain in that immortal feature of loveliness and perfection fashioned by the blind poet.

6

Samson and Christ

In *Paradise Lost,* then, Milton substitutes for the ontological ascent of Neoplatonism the historical and psychological ascent of Christianity from "shadowy Types to Truth," the Garden to the "Paradise within," the Law to the Gospel, the carnal to the spiritual, outward observance to inward holiness. Physical images, like the types of the Old Testament, represent a stage in the history of man's religious development; their function ceases with the coming of Christ, who is the true Image of God. In *Paradise Lost,* as we have seen, Milton assigns to unfallen nature the limited symbolic function of foreshadowing the Fall; after the Fall the sacred history and the ceremonies instituted by God foreshadow dimly and obscurely the promised Redemption; with the coming of Christ the symbolic drama is at an end, and there is only the Word and the Spirit. "Believe it, wondrous doctors, all corporeal resemblances of inward holiness and beauty are now past."[1] The whole system of symbolic correspondences so luxuriantly developed by medieval Christianity and adopted at least in part by seventeenth-century Anglicanism Milton simply rejects

1. *Reason of Church Government,* II.ii, *SM,* p. 528.

as irrelevant at best and the work of Satan at worst. Even in his doctrine of the sacraments, which most Protestants regarded as a gracious concession to man's sensuous nature, Milton emphasizes the function of the word and minimizes the physical image. This same movement from outer to inner occurs in the development of Milton's attitude toward contemporary history. The youthful confidence that God was leading His Chosen People, the English, out of the Egypt of prelacy to the Promised Land of the "one right discipline" gave way to the realization that the English in 1660 were "choosing them a captain back for Egypt";[2] in 1666 he could say that "One's country is wherever it is well with one."[3] The man who once signed himself Johannes Miltonius, Anglus, and added the motto *Coelum non animum muto dum trans mare curro* had apparently come to regard the England of his early apocalyptic vision as akin to the types and shadows of the Old Testament, and even nationality was spiritualized into a purely inward reality.[4]

Few would deny that this is the general pattern of Milton's development and that it culminates in *Paradise Lost* and especially in *Paradise Regained*. But what about *Samson Agonistes*? Unless we adopt the theory that *Samson* was written in the 1640s, which almost all recent critics

2. *Ready and Easy Way, SM*, p. 914.

3. Letter to Peter Heimbach (15 Aug. 1666), *SM*, p. 1096.

4. See the excellent discussion in Michael Fixler, *Milton and the Kingdoms of God* (Evanston, Northwestern University Press, 1964), esp. pp. 213–20.

seem unwilling to do,[5] we are faced with the task of explaining why one of Milton's last poems seems to run counter to the whole tenor of his mature thought as expressed in his two epics.

One way of doing this is simply to assert that *Samson* represents a development beyond *Paradise Regained* and in a sense a return to earlier beliefs. Harold Fisch regards *Samson* as Milton's central poetic utterance. It is, he says, "the most completely realized of Milton's poems and also . . . the most genuinely Hebraic."[6] *Paradise Lost* and *Paradise Regained* do not, according to Fisch, represent the logical development of Milton's thought. Reversing the usual argument that rejection of religious images entails rejection of poetic imagery, Fisch says that Milton "was not in his deepest nature the enemy of ceremonial. He was no iconoclast like Luther. We need only think of his festive and ceremonious style, so different from the austerities of typical Puritan writing." If political events in England had taken a different course, if King Charles had not "betrayed as he did the integrity of the nation as a sacred community," one could imagine Milton, "far from urging the separation of Church, State, and Crown, . . . fighting for their unification as a necessary prerequisite for that complete religious life which includes the whole Man, his body and soul, his political as well as his ecclesiastical affilia-

5. A cogent refutation of the arguments for an early date may be found in Ernest Sirluck, "Milton's Idle Right Hand," *JEGP, 60* (1961), Appendix I, 773–81.
6. *Jerusalem and Albion*, p. 140.

183

tions." In short, "Milton was drawn in his deepest nature to that integration of Power and Goodness which in political terms would be represented by an active combination of the forces of Church and State, not a theocracy on Genevan lines but one which allowed for a greater expression of national culture and tradition and a more festively royal and religious ceremonial." Such a union of power and goodness is found in *Samson,* where "action and self-control are united in a definitely Hebraic fashion."[7]

A much more common way of explaining *Samson Agonistes* is to minimize its differences from the other two poems of Milton's maturity, in short, to assert that it is a Christian poem. Thus we are told that its spirit is "religious and Christian"; it is "a classical tragedy with a Christian theme and outlook"; it is a "remarkable blend of Greek form with Christian content"; Samson himself is "an heroic figure as conspicuously modern, Christian, and Miltonic as it is Hebraic"; *Samson Agonistes* is really *Christus Agonistes,* and the agony of Samson is a "surrogate for the unbloody sacrifice of the Mass."[8]

The fact that Milton was an avowed Christian poet gives these views a good deal of antecedent probability; still, *Samson Agonistes* does not read like a Christian play. It is

7. Ibid., pp. 162, 163, 140–41.

8. Walter Clyde Curry, "*Samson Agonistes* Yet Again," *SR,* 32 (1924), 351; A. S. P. Woodhouse, "Tragic Effect in *Samson Agonistes,*" *UTQ,* 28 (1959), 222; Kenneth Muir, *John Milton* (London, 1955), p. 183; E. M. Clark, "Milton's Conception of Samson," *University of Texas Studies in English, 8* (1928), 99; T. S. K. Scott-Craig, "Concerning Milton's Samson," *RN, 5* (1952), 46–47.

very difficult to transmute the muscular Samson into a Christian athlete, and even more difficult to make Christians of Manoa and the Chorus, from whose mouths proceed all the reflections on the meaning of Samson's tragedy. Critics who are not themselves Christians, or who wrote before Christian orthodoxy once again became intellectually respectable, have felt no compulsion to Christianize the play. James Holly Hanford went so far as to say that *Samson* proves that Milton did not think that Christ's sacrifice was a necessary instrument of salvation; even Christ's example, it appears, might be dispensed with for those who enjoy a direct and special relation with the Divine. More recently Arnold Stein's careful analysis contains not a single reference to Christ or Christianity (though his interpretation, as I hope to show, is the most profoundly Christian of all).[9]

How one relates *Samson* to *Paradise Lost* and *Paradise Regained* depends to some extent on whether one regards the play as Christian, but there are problems enough in either case. Tillyard sees in it evidence that Milton had regained his faith in action after the quietism of *Paradise Regained;* Maynard Mack sees no conflict but rather a reconciliation of the competing ideals of action and contemplation. Woodhouse does not think a work so divergent from *Paradise Regained* in "doctrine, temper, and tone" could have been written at the same time and consequently

9. James Holly Hanford, "*Samson Agonistes* and Milton in Old Age," *Studies in Shakespeare, Milton and Donne* (New York, 1925), p. 177; Arnold Stein, *Heroic Knowledge* (Minneapolis, 1957).

dates *Samson* in 1660–61, the period of Milton's greatest disillusionment. Others, however, see it as a kind of companion piece to the two epics in that it presents a "pattern-hero" who differs from Abdiel and Christ only in being more fully human and whose regeneration is thus a more compelling example for the fallen sons of Adam.[10]

It is ironic that a work whose simplicity and straightforwardness are often commented on should have given rise to such divergent and even antithetical judgments. There are those, no doubt, who would attribute this fact to the well-known tendency of Milton scholars toward special pleading—the problem of belief seems to arise in an especially acute form when Milton is being discussed—but I would attribute it rather to a failure to realize that *Samson Agonistes is* complex in a special way. It is complex because it is both Hebraic and Christian in much the same way that the Old Testament may be considered both Hebraic and Christian. Just as the seventeenth-century Christian was instructed to read the Old Testament with an eye to "Christ and his mysteries," so would Milton expect *Samson Agonistes* to be read. It must be read, in a word, typologically.

What has typology to do with Samson? Milton nowhere discusses Samson as a type of Christ, and critics as different

---

10. E. M. W. Tillyard, *Milton* (London, 1930), p. 328; Maynard Mack, ed., *Milton* (Englewood Cliffs, 1950), p. 28; A. S. P. Woodhouse, "*Samson Agonistes* and Milton's Experience," *Transactions of the Royal Society of Canada,* 3d Ser., *43,* Sec. 2 (1949), 157–58; M. M. Mahood, *Poetry and Humanism* (New Haven, 1950), p. 211.

in their assumptions and methods as Hanford, Krouse, Woodhouse, and MacCallum[11] agree that Milton made little or no use of the traditional typological parallels in his play. It is true, of course, that there are no explicit references to Samson as a type of Christ. How could there be when the words of the drama are confined to Old Testament actors? The meaning of a type cannot be known until the antitype has been revealed, and Samson, Manoa, and the Chorus knew nothing of Christ. That there is an implicit foreshadowing of Christ in Milton's Samson I shall discuss in a moment; however, it is even more important for an understanding of Milton's conception of Samson to recognize the differences between Samson and Christ, for it is essential to the whole system of typology that the type be different from as well as similar to the antitype.

The major differences between Samson and the Christ of *Paradise Regained* can be summed up as action vs. passion and letter (or flesh) vs. spirit (or word). Just after Harapha leaves, the Chorus exults in the return of Samson's heroic vigor:

> Oh how comely it is and how reviving
> To the Spirits of just men long opprest!
> When God into the hands of thir deliverer
> Puts invincible might
> To quell the mighty of the Earth, th' oppressor,

11. F. Michael Krouse, *Milton's Samson and the Tradition* (Princeton, 1949); MacCallum, "Milton and Figurative Interpretation of the Bible."

187

> The brute and boist'rous force of violent men
> Hardy and industrious to support
> Tyrannic power, but raging to pursue
> The righteous and all such as honor Truth.
>
> (ll. 1268–76)

Mindful of Samson's plight, however, the Chorus goes on to suggest that his vocation may be that of the patient sufferer:

> But patience is more oft the exercise
> Of Saints, the trial of thir fortitude,
> Making them each his own Deliverer,
> And Victor over all
> That tyranny or fortune can inflict.
> Either of these is in thy lot,
> *Samson,* with might endu'd
> Above the Sons of men; but sight bereav'd
> May chance to number thee with those
> Whom Patience finally must crown.   (ll. 1287–96)

The vaguely Christian connotations of the words "saints" and "patience" should not blind us to the essentially stoic quality of the idea of victory over "fortune," "lot," and "chance." Even if one should insist on regarding this passage as Christian, it is clear that the Chorus finally regards Samson as an active, not a passive, hero: "O dearly bought revenge, yet glorious!" Manoa echoes the Chorus' thought:

> *Samson* hath quit himself
> Like *Samson,* and heroicly hath finish'd

A life Heroic, on his Enemies
Fully reveng'd hath left them years of mourning.

(ll. 1709–12)

Samson's death was representative of his life, and his
memory will inflame the breasts of the valiant youth of
Israel "To matchless valor, and adventures high" (l. 1740).

One such valiant youth was the young Jesus of *Paradise
Regained*. Although He does not mention Samson in His
soliloquy in the desert, the example of an earlier deliverer
springs readily to mind when He says

> yet this not all
> To which my Spirit aspir'd; victorious deeds
> Flam'd in my heart, heroic acts; one while
> To rescue *Israel* from the *Roman* yoke,
> Then to subdue and quell o'er all the earth
> Brute violence and proud Tyrannic pow'r,
> Till truth were freed, and equity restor'd.

(I.214–20)

These are precisely the terms the Chorus used in the
passage about the active hero quoted above, and Samson
too had spoken of his own "great exploits" (l. 32) and
"mightiest deeds" (l. 638) and of the promise that he
"Should *Israel* from *Philistian* yoke deliver" (l. 39). The
similarities, however, only heighten the great and significant difference: the aspiration to victorious deeds is an
early stage of Christ's spiritual development; it is, in fact,
one of the temptations of Satan, who is the great celebrator

189

of heroic action in *Paradise Regained*. Satan tells the devils that Christ is adorned with "amplitude of mind to greatest Deeds" (II.139); His mind, more exalted than Solomon's, is "set wholly on th' accomplishment / Of greatest things" (II.207–08). Later he tells Christ, "all thy heart is set on high designs, / High actions" (II.410–11), and the heroes he proposes for imitation are all men of action—Alexander, Scipio Africanus, Pompey, Julius Caesar, and Judas Maccabaeus, who retired to the desert with arms. One would hardly be surprised if Satan were to add the name of Samson to this list. Satan's understanding of Christ's role as the deliverer of Israel is similar to Samson's understanding of his own role, and when Satan appeals to Christ's sense of zeal and duty by recounting the abominations inflicted on Israel by the Romans, he echoes the Chorus in *Samson* when it speaks of "Tyrannic power . . . raging to pursue / The righteous and all such as honor Truth" (ll. 1275–76).

Samson's inability to rise to Christ's contempt for "ostentation vain of fleshly arm" (III.387) is underlined by Milton in the Harapha episode. Whether or not Harapha's visit is regarded as a temptation, it is clear that Samson's response is seriously flawed. Wholly admirable is his trust in the living God, his willingness to acknowledge that God has inflicted these indignities on him justly; less admirable, at best, is his eagerness to engage Harapha in single combat, his pathetic belief that by clubbing Harapha to death he will demonstrate the glory of God. The language of chivalric combat used by both Samson and Harapha[12] places this encounter at a vast moral distance from the "great duel, not of arms" in which Christ engages the Father of all the giants of the earth. Samson, it is true, has purified his motives since the time when "swoll'n with pride" he walked about "like a petty God . . . admir'd of all and dreaded" (ll. 529–32). But while purity of heart is a necessary part of the "wisdom" that vanquishes "hellish wiles" (I.175), it is not enough. After all, some of the motives that Satan proposed to Christ were beyond reproach.

A more fundamental contrast between Samson and Christ is comprehended in Michael's lines:

So Law appears imperfet, and but giv'n
With purpose to resign them in full time
Up to a better Cov'nant, disciplin'd
From shadowy Types to Truth, from Flesh to Spirit.

Throughout his life, as we have seen, Milton opposed the literalism and carnality of the Old Testament to the spirituality of the New. It is the basis of his attack on the bishops, whom he calls Judaizers and whose altars and candles at noon he says were "superstitions fetched from paganism or Jewism."[13] The Jews of the Old Testament, according to Milton, were content to remain in the letter

12. Ralph Nash, "Chivalric Themes in *Samson Agonistes*," in *Studies in Honor of John Wilcox* (Detroit, 1958), pp. 23–38.

13. *The Likeliest Means To Remove Hirelings, SM*, p. 886.

of the law and did not realize, for example, that the ceremonial vestments were merely typical foreshadowings of the inward purity of Christians.

In *Paradise Regained* it is primarily Satan who represents the fleshly, literalistic Old Testament point of view.[14] Someone wittily observed that the trouble with Satan is that he cannot recognize a metaphor. The most obvious example is his failure to understand the significance of the Dove. When he was at the baptism of Christ, he tells his followers, he saw Heaven unfold her crystal doors and on Christ's head "A perfect Dove descend, whate'er it meant." Christ, on the other hand, knows what it meant:

> But as I rose out of the laving stream,
> Heaven open'd her eternal doors, from whence
> The Spirit descended on me like a Dove.
>
> (I.280–82)

In the temptations that follow, Christ's strategy with Satan is to internalize and spiritualize Satan's terms by turning them into metaphors. And Satan is so literalistic that he cannot understand a metaphor even when it is explained to him. To his suggestion that Christ turn stones into bread to provide Himself and others in the wilderness with food, Christ replies, "Is it not written . . . Man lives not by Bread only, but each Word / Proceeding from the mouth of God?" A little later He contrasts God's Word to

14. This topic is developed in brilliant detail by Barbara Kiefer Lewalski, *Milton's Brief Epic: The Genre, Meaning, and Art of* Paradise Regained (Providence and London, 1966), passim.

the words that proceed from Satan's oracles: "For lying is thy sustenance, thy food." Satan returns next morning, however, to appeal to Christ's physical hunger, telling the devils, "And now I know he hungers where no food / Is to be found, in the wide Wilderness." But Christ is "fed with better thoughts" and is "hung'ring more to do [his] Father's will" (II.258–59). When He tells Satan He has no need of food, the arch-literalist is baffled. "How hast thou hunger then?" he asks (II.321) and proceeds to display his ludicrous baroque banquet. Christ counters with an oblique reference to the Eucharist:[15]

> I can at will, doubt not, as soon as thou,
> Command a Table in this Wilderness,
> And call swift flights of Angels ministrant
> Array'd in Glory on my cup to attend,
>
> (II.383–86)

and ends with a contemptuous question, "And with my hunger what hast thou to do?" (II.389).

In the temptation of the kingdoms which follows, Satan clings to his literalistic Old Testament interpretation of the role of the Messiah. Christ tells him, before the temptation is well under way, that he who reigns within himself is more a king; that to guide nations in the way of truth is yet more kingly; and that "to give a Kingdom hath been thought / Greater and nobler done, and to lay down / Far more magnanimous than to assume" (II.481–83). But Satan does not hear; he merely shifts his ground from

15. Martz, *The Paradise Within*, p. 187.

means to motives, appealing to Christ's sense of glory and then to his zeal and duty "to free / Thy Country from her Heathen servitude" (III.175–76). Christ's conception of spiritual liberty and servitude is far beyond Satan's ken, however:

> Should I of these the liberty regard,
> Who freed, as to their ancient Patrimony,
> Unhumbl'd, unrepentant, unreform'd,
> Headlong would follow, and to thir Gods perhaps
> Of *Bethel* and of *Dan?*   (III.427–31)

But Satan persists, suggesting that Christ might ascend the throne of Tiberius and "A victor people free from servile yoke" (IV.102). "What wise and valiant man would seek to free / These thus degenerate, by themselves enslav'd," asks Christ, "Or could of inward slaves make outward free?" (IV.142–45). The baffled Satan makes one last effort of the imagination. Christ seems "otherwise inclin'd / Than to a worldly Crown," and Satan suggests to Him that, as His empire must extend, "So let extend thy mind o'er all the world," ruling the Gentiles by persuasion (IV.212–32). This is the furthest Satan's mind will stretch, however, and when Christ rejects the learning of Athens, Satan admits he does not understand whether Christ's kingdom will be "Real or Allegoric" (IV.390). The joke is on Satan, as Northrop Frye has shown, for Christ's kingdom, which is allegoric to Satan, is the only real kingdom there is.[16]

16. Northrop Frye, "The Typology of *Paradise Regained*," MP, 53 (1956), 231.

One way of defining Christ's strategy in *Paradise Regained* would be to call it a purification of the word: "In the beginning was the Word, and the Word was made flesh." Milton would add to this formula, "The Word was made flesh so that flesh might become word."[17] In *Paradise Lost* when Christ incarnates Himself, He does not lessen or degrade His nature, but rather raises human nature to the level of divinity; when Satan incarnates himself in the serpent, he merely imbrutes his own essence.

In *Samson Agonistes*, there is no such metaphorical activity; at the most, stones are turned into bread, but physical hunger is not transmuted into spiritual hunger. The two major motives of blindness and delivery from bondage receive only a limited metaphorical extension that falls far short of Christ's achievement in *Paradise Regained*. Samson, for example, has enough insight to recognize that his present servitude is not so ignominious as his servitude to Dalila, and he can see that the Israelites were brought to servitude by their vices and hence prefer "Bondage with ease" to "strenuous liberty" (l. 271), but he still thinks it possible of "inward slaves [to] make outward free" *(PR, IV.145)*. The insights of the Chorus are on a lower level: it regards Samson's blindness as a "Prison within Prison" (l. 153) and suggests that the man who can patiently endure what chance inflicts is the deliverer of himself. Manoa's apprehension is the most earthly and literalistic of all as he pathetically and ironically bustles

17. See above, Chap. 5, pp. 178–80.

off to arrange for Samson's ransom. His final recognition that "death who sets all free / Hath paid his ransom now and full discharge" (ll. 1572–73) rises no higher than the pagan conception of death as release from affliction. All these attempts to purify the ideas of bondage and deliverance remain within the limited moral and spiritual vision of paganism and Old Testament Judaism; nowhere is there a realization that because of Adam's sin man is in bondage to Satan and that Christ is his only deliverer, that it is Christ's death alone that sets all men free, and that to the faithful death is "the Gate of Life" (PL, XII.571).

In the same manner the theme of blindness receives at most a moral purification. Manoa characteristically hopes for a miracle, the literal restoration of Samson's sight. The Chorus refers to Samson's "inward eyes" (l. 1689), but it does not suggest that he can tell of things invisible to mortal sight. Samson's insight, like his insight about his bondage to Dalila, is that his present blindness is not so bad as when he "saw not how degenerately [he] serv'd" (l. 419). When Samson's limited awareness is compared with Milton's exalted spiritualizing of blindness in the invocation to Book III of Paradise Lost, it seems justifiable to assume that Samson suffers a kind of spiritual, as well as physical, blindness.

The contrast between the old dispensation of the Letter and the new dispensation of the Spirit is deliberately heightened by Milton's technique of putting into the mouths of the characters words that almost automatically call for a metaphorical interpretation by the Christian reader. One of my students saw in the following lines an oblique allusion to the Crucifixion:

> O dark, dark, dark, amid the blaze of noon,
> Irrecoverably dark, total Eclipse
> Without all hope of day! (ll. 80–82)

If that seems too private, more than one commentator has heard Christian overtones in the following lines of Manoa:

> Reject not then what offer'd means, who knows
> But God hath set before us, to return thee
> Home to thy country and his sacred house,
> (ll. 516–18)

> I however
> Must not omit a Father's timely care
> To prosecute the means of thy deliverance
> By ransom or how else. (ll. 601–04)

The most obvious example is the Chorus' comparison of Samson with the phoenix:

> So virtue giv'n for lost,
> Deprest, and overthrown, as seem'd,
> Like that self-begott'n bird
> In the *Arabian* woods embost,
> That no second knows nor third,
> And lay erewhile a Holocaust,
> From out her ashy womb now teem'd,
> Revives, reflourishes, then vigorous most
> When most unactive deem'd,

> And though her body die, her fame survives,
> A secular bird ages of lives.   (ll. 1697–1707)

The comparison of Christ with the phoenix was a Christian commonplace; here, significantly, the phoenix is not used as a symbol of personal immortality, but as a symbol of the immortality of fame.

Alongside such terms, whose Christian significance provides an ironic counterpoint to the literal significance intended by the speakers, are found words that can be regarded only as Old Testament or pagan. The emphasis on revenge at the end of the play is the notorious example; equally pagan is the Chorus' reliance on the concepts of fortune, chance, and lot in the famous passage on patience already quoted. It is hard to avoid the conclusion that Milton, far from trying to Christianize *Samson Agonistes,* was at some pains to maintain the integrity of his Old Testament materials. Instead of collapsing Samson and Christ, he is concerned with measuring the distance between the various levels of awareness (represented by Manoa, the Chorus, and Samson) possible to those living under the old dispensation and the level of awareness revealed by Christ in *Paradise Regained.*[18]

In what respect, then, is Milton's Samson like Christ? Did Milton simply turn his back on the whole tradition of Christian exegesis of the Samson story? With much of that tradition he no doubt had little sympathy. One cannot think that Milton regarded the carrying off of the gates of

18. Cf. my discussion of *Lycidas* in Chap. 1, above.

Azzah as a type of the harrowing of Hell, or the jawbone of the ass as a type of the Gospel, or Samson's locks as the rays of heavenly contemplation. Certainly no such fanciful resemblances found their way into *Samson Agonistes*. In the list of parallels between Samson and Christ given in Thomas Hayne's *The General View of the Holy Scriptures,* however, there is a significant item which, taken in conjunction with Arnold Stein's analysis of the meaning of Samson's agon, fully reveals Milton's intention. The last of Hayne's parallels reads (in part) as follows: "Christs Divinitie permitting it, he was bound, led to the Judgement hall, mocked." In the opposite column: "The spirit of God, which strengthened Sampson, permitting, he was bound, led away, mocked."[19]

Samson's agonized consciousness that he is an object of scorn and mockery is a motive that runs all through the play. As early as line 34 he complains that he has been made the "scorn and gaze" of his enemies; a little later he says he is exposed

> To daily fraud, contempt, abuse and wrong,
> Within doors, or without, still as a fool,
> In power of others, never in my own.   (ll. 76–78)

When he hears the Chorus approaching he thinks it is his enemies "who come to stare / At my affliction, and perhaps to insult" (ll. 112–13), and he reverts to this topic at least twelve more times in the course of the play. The

19. Thomas Hayne, *The General View of the Holy Scriptures* (London, 1640), p. 218, reproduced in Krouse, *Milton's Samson,* facing p. 69.

climax of this theme is reached when Samson refuses to
go with the Philistine officer:

> Have they not Sword-players, and ev'ry sort
> Of Gymnic Artists, Wrestlers, Riders, Runners,
> Jugglers and Dancers, Antics, Mummers, Mimics,
> But they must pick mee out with shackles tir'd,
> And over-labor'd at thir public Mill,
> To make them sport with blind activity?
>
>   . . .
>
> Can they think me so broken, so debas'd
> With corporal servitude, that my mind ever
> Will condescend to such absurd commands?
> Although thir drudge, to be thir fool or jester,
> And in my midst of sorrow and heart-grief
> To show them feats, and play before thir god,
> The worst of all indignities, yet on me
> Join'd with extreme contempt? I will not come.
>
>   (ll. 1323–28, 1335–42)

But he does come, and, as Stein so finely says, the man
who failed as the athlete of God succeeds as the fool of
God.[20] Samson himself is not conscious of the significance
of his new role; he has not learned that it is humiliation
that exalts. Earlier he had acknowledged that the indignities heaped on him by Harapha were inflicted justly by
God; here there is no indication in the text that Samson
attaches any moral or spiritual significance to his willing-

20. *Heroic Knowledge,* p. 196.

ness to suffer public humiliation at the Philistine games.
On the contrary, he obviously still thinks of himself as the
athlete of God:

> If there be aught of presage in the mind,
> This day will be remarkable in my life
> By some great act, or of my days the last.
>
> (ll. 1387–89)

And it is as act, not as passion, that Manoa and the Chorus
regard Samson's victory. He has revenged himself on his
enemies and heroically has finished a life heroic. Only in
a few words of the Messenger is there a glimpse of the
Samson who might have been: "He patient but undaunted
where they led him, / Came to the place" (ll. 1623–24).
But not to the place called Golgotha. Even in this essential
parallel between Samson and Christ one is acutely aware
of the difference between the "faithful champion" who
destroys his enemies and the Savior who forgives and
redeems His.

The harshness of the contrast between Samson's ethic
and Christ's may be mitigated by regarding the destruction
of the Philistines as a foreshadowing of God's terrible
judgment on evil and of the Last Judgment in particular.
Such an interpretation, however, robs Samson of his exis-
tential reality and makes the play a ghostly paradigm. If,
on the other hand, Samson is viewed first of all as a concrete individual living in a concrete historical situation,
then his significance for the Christian reader lies primarily
in his inability to measure up to the heroic norm delin-

eated in *Paradise Regained*. For it is humiliation that exalts, not the ruin of a pagan temple. Although he dimly foreshadows the humiliation of his Savior, Samson remains blind to the spiritual significance of his suffering. Living before the age of the Word, he cannot see the lively image of Christ. Neither he, nor Manoa, nor the Chorus can know that they must all remain in bondage until the death of One Who will in truth, not in shadow, prosecute the means of their deliverance and return them home to their Father's house.

Index

INDEX

INDEX

"Il Penseroso," 1, 17; "L'Allegro," 1; "Lycidas," 6 f.; "Nativity Ode," 1, 6, 61

Areopagitica, 179; *Christian Doctrine*, 49, 84, 113, 179; *Colasterion*, 68; *Doctrine and Discipline of Divorce*, 82; *Letter to Peter Heimbach*, 182; *Likeliest Means*, 50–51, 191; *Of Reformation*, 52, 109, 144; *Ready and Easy Way*, 182; *Reason of Church Government*, 49–51, 81, 108, 181; *Tenure of Kings and Magistrates*, 71; *Treatise of Civil Power*, 71

Paradise Lost, 85–180 (chaps. 4 and 5) passim; Abdiel, 111–12; Adam, 49, 58, 67–69, 84, 101 f., 119, 142, 148 f., 163 f.; Christ as symbolizing center of, 53, 83–84, 121–22, 178–79 *(see also* 130 f.); Eve, 58, 67–69, 84, 103 f., 138, 142, 148 f., 163 f.; Garden, 60, 84, 102 f., 121–22, 144; metaphor in, 55 f. and passim; Michael, 49, 107, 124; modes of discourse in, 82–83; Moloch, 123; narrator, 18–19, 52, 56, 81; Raphael, 59, 74, 87, 101, 110, 111 n., 119 f., 142, 147–48, 152; Satan, 57–58, 84, 87, 103, 123–24, 150 f., 165; Sin and Death, 61, 150; War in Heaven, 87, 110 f.

Paradise Regained, 20, 106, 123–24, 181–202 (chap. 6) passim; *Samson Agonistes*, 20, 181–202 (chap. 6) passim

Mitchell, W. Fraser, 169

More, Henry, 46 f., 102
Mott, F. L., 160
Mozart, 8
Muir, Kenneth, 184 n.
Murdock, Kenneth, 168 f.

Nash, Ralph, 191 n.
Nemmers, E. E., 127 n.
Neoplatonism, 2, 16–17, 19, 46, 60 f., 75, 83, 85–144 (chap. 4) passim, 173
Nicholas of Cusa, 93, 128
Nicholson, Marjorie Hope, 64 f., 129

Origen, 23, 26, 39, 48
Orpheus, 7, 9, 17, 75
Osgood, Charles G., 17 n.

Page, B. S., 91 n.
Panofsky, Erwin, 147, 170 n.
Patrides, C. A., 1 n.
Patterson, F. A., 67 n.
Paul, St., 28–29, 33, 39, 95–97, 158–59, 166
Perkins, William, 48 n., 136–37, 176
Philo Judaeus, 99, 102
Pico della Mirandola, 24, 93, 117–18, 147–48
Plato, 88, 89, 114, 125 n., 145, 155 n., 158, 160 n., 173 n.
Plotinus, 91, 102, 114–16, 122, 138, 145–46
Plutarch, 72
Pontifex, Mark, 139 n.
Potter, George R., 155 n.
Prat, Fernand, 100
Psychomachia, 22
Purdy, A. C., 98

206

INDEX